You'll Never Blue Ball in This Town Again

One Woman's Painfully Funny Quest to Give It Up

Heather McDonald

A Touchstone Book
Published by Simon & Schuster
New York   London   Toronto   Sydney

 Touchstone
A Division of Simon & Schuster, Inc.
1230 Avenue of the Americas
New York, NY 10020

This memoir presents my recollections of twenty years of my life, filtered through the prism of memory, embarrassment, and humor. Names have been changed; characters and events combined, compressed, and reordered.

First Touchstone trade paperback edition June 2010

TOUCHSTONE and colophon are registered trademarks of Simon & Schuster, Inc.

For information about special discounts for bulk purchases, please contact Simon & Schuster Special Sales at 1-866-506-1949 or business@simonandschuster.com.

The Simon & Schuster Speakers Bureau can bring authors to your live event. For more information or to book an event, contact the Simon & Schuster Speakers Bureau at 1-866-248-3049 or visit our website at www.simonspeakers.com.

Designed by Ruth Lee-Mui

Manufactured in the United States of America

10 9 8 7 6 5 4

Library of Congress Cataloging-in-Publication Data

McDonald, Heather.
  You'll never blue ball in this town again : one woman's painfully funny quest to give it up / by Heather McDonald.
     p. cm.
  "A Touchstone book."
  1. Women comedians—United States—Biography. 2. Sex—Humor.
3. Virginity—Social aspects—United States. 4. Television personalities—United States—Biography. I. Title.
  PN2287.M5455A3 2010
  792.702'8092—dc22
  [B]   2010009462

ISBN 978-1-4391-7628-3
ISBN 978-1-4391-7630-6 (ebook)

To my funny and fabulous parents, Bob and Pam,
I love you both. Now turn the TV back on, you don't need
to read this.

Contents

 Prologue

Finally, late one night on the phone I got up the courage to tell Kevin that I was a virgin. I absolutely hated saying the word *virgin* aloud because it always made me think of the Virgin Mary, who in my opinion never got enough props for giving birth without having sex or an epidural in a manger with some hay up her ass all while three strange men whom she'd never met before insisted on being there just because they brought some frankincense and myrrh. But I managed to tell him, and Kevin was the first and the last guy who thought it was a good thing. He was confident he would be my first, but he wasn't going to rush me, which was good because I was in no rush to do it with him. The only rush that mattered was spring sorority rush.

Kevin and I had these long dry humping make-out sessions. While fully clothed, we French kissed and I did the grind on his hard penis. One night, Kevin told me on the phone that I was blue balling him so badly that he was at risk for contracting testicular cancer. I felt terrible. The next night, I was listening to *Love Line* on the radio. Dr. Drew Pinsky and Adam Corolla were the cohosts while people called in to get advice on their love problems. I called in and got through to the screener.

"Welcome to *Love Line*. What's your question?" asked the screener.

"Well, I'm a nineteen-year-old virgin and . . ."

He cut me off. "Really, a nineteen-year-old virgin?"

I felt like he thought he had struck gold or something.

"Yes, and my boyfriend says that I blue ball him so much he could get testicular cancer. I want to ask Dr. Drew if that is possible."

"OK, turn down your radio and hang on the line," he said to me as I promptly sat on the bed and waited on the line.

Wow, I'm going to be on the radio. I had never in my life even attempted to be the sixteenth caller on the radio to win U2 tickets.

Dr. Drew immediately got on the line and assured me that you cannot get testicular cancer from being blue balled. But Adam was impressed that a guy had the inventiveness to guilt a girl into putting out by telling her she was causing him cancer. Well, this certainly made me feel a lot better knowing that unlike the tobacco industry, Heather McDonald was no longer on the American Cancer Society hit list. . . .

1 Can't a Girl Dress Like a Hooker, Dance Like a Stripper, and Kiss Like a Porn Star and Still Be a Nineteen-Year-Old Virgin?

Do you ever find yourself in your office daydreaming of an old crush and wondering what your life would have been like with him, especially on the days when your husband isn't treating you like the princess you still are? Suddenly the crush comes to mind and you decide to Internet stalk him to find out if he is still single or to see how ugly his wife is or what your kids may have looked like with him. Well, Kevin O'Sullivan is the guy I Google and search on Facebook, MySpace, LinkedIn, Classmates, and so on. When my husband is not being nice to me, he refuses to help me on the computer in my attempt to track down this old flame of mine.

With a name like Kevin O'Sullivan, I knew he was Irish.

In fact, his parents were from Ireland: the land of potatoes; four-leaf clovers; leprechauns and Lucky Charms cereal; and, of course, famine and bloodshed. He went to Arizona State, where I was visiting my friend Suzanne, but his family lived in Pasadena, which is just outside of LA, but at least an hour from my home in Woodland Hills. We went through the usual college pre-hookup-meet-and-greet of "What's your major? Dorm? High school? What was your SAT? Is there a history of cancer in your family? How about acne?"

With Kevin the conversation was really easy, and the alcohol helped. I don't think I ever saw the bottom of my red plastic cup. Fraternity guys are trained to never allow a sorority sister's drink to run out. They're such gentlemen in that way.

At about one a.m., it was time for us to leave. Suzanne was from Arizona and we were crashing at her parents' house, so we couldn't be too late. Kevin asked for my number and I asked for his. I loved having the guy's number. At the time, my Heather philosophy was that these guys always lose the little pieces of paper with the numbers scribbled on them; they must lose them, or what other explanation is there for them not calling? I couldn't risk the possibility that my precious phone number might be held hostage in the crevice of a futon for months and by the time it was rescued the guy would have no recollection of who I was.

If you can believe it, in the nineties there were no Black-Berrys or iPhones or Palm Pilots, so the potential boyfriend could not program my digits in his telecommunicative device. By getting his number I had control if I chose to call him. He said he'd be back in Pasadena over Thanksgiving and we should go out then. I was going to hold him to it and that's why I kept his number safe in my Velcro Louis Vuitton knockoff wallet. I also transcribed it into two different notebooks in two different locations just in case I was approached by a mugger while walking to my car and I couldn't reach my mace or kick him in the groin while yelling "fire" (I was told "fire" gets more of a response than "rape") and he successfully grabbed my purse.

Like Oprah says, "Never go to the second crime location," even if it means a potential boyfriend's phone number might be lost forever. I also decided to always keep a bottled water and granola bar in my car so that when the big earthquake strikes and a freeway collapses on my car, I can eventually tell Oprah, "And even though there was only a small pocket of air, I managed to reach down and get that water and granola bar until help arrived." Oprah always tears up at a good story about survival and rationing one granola bar over a period of ten days.

Thanksgiving weekend rolled around and I left USC, where I was in my sophomore year, for the long forty-six-minute drive home to the Valley. The Wednesday before Thanksgiving Day is always a great party night. People don't have to work the next day, and some are staying, like me, at their parents' house. I loved flopping into my double bed with its pink ruffled canapé top, which, by the way, does not work like a bunk bed. My sister and I learned this the hard way. I would lie among my stuffed elephants and panda bears, which were impossible to cuddle because they were all won by my dad from various trips to Six

Flags and therefore synthetic, and watch my junior varsity cheer-leading ribbons spinning around my room before I passed out. This memory repeated itself every Thanksgiving. It just always screamed "autumn" to me.

Around six p.m. on Thanksgiving, with some Blue Nun wine and tryptophan in my bloodstream, I decided to call Kevin O'Sullivan and see if he still wanted to take me out that week-end. Needless to say, he hadn't called me. I retrieved the number from my wallet and dialed. It was his home number and an Irish woman answered, which freaked me out because any Irish woman sounds like a nun to me. My heart was already beating because I was calling a boy, and now I was having flashbacks of my fourth-grade math teacher, Sister Therese.

"Yes, is Kevin there please?" I asked as politely as I could, thinking she could ask me to solve a long division problem at any moment.

"One moment dear," she replied.

"Hello?" Kevin said.

"Oh, hi. This is Heather. I met you at the ATO party a while back. I go to USC and . . ." He cut me off.

"Of course. How are you, Heather?" he asked. The rest of the conversation was easy, yet my heart still managed to beat at an excessive rate. Whenever I was on the phone at my parents' house I never knew when my dad would start yelling about something so loud that the person on the other end would hear, "Don't get your tit in a wringer about the blood. Just get me the goddamn Band-Aids!" When that happened, I would immediately hang up, and then when the house was quiet again I'd call back and say, "What's up with your phone, we just got disconnected, that's so weird, you should have that checked out." We made plans for Kevin to pick me up on Friday night at my parents' house and decided we would go out in Woodland Hills.

The next day, my sister Shannon and I went shopping. I love when you shop for a new outfit and then have plans to wear it that very night, provided the idiotic salesgirl doesn't forget to remove the security tag. When that happened to me, I called the store in a panic demanding that they send someone from Forever 21 immediately to my home with the security removal gun and take care of the situation or I would file a lawsuit on the grounds of intentional infliction of emotional distress. When the salesgirl made a sarcastic remark about how they don't make house calls for purchases under twenty-nine dollars, I attempted to remove the tag myself and went out that night looking like I'd been shot by a blue paintball gun.

Being a virgin never conflicted with the way I dressed. My philosophy at the time was: If I don't show it, how will people know I have it? So the shorter and tighter the outfit the better. Shannon was not as risqué and didn't always agree with my clothing. I was so confident with my Forever 21 purchases that even as an aspiring attorney she wasn't able to convince me that cleavage and upper thigh should not both be the focal points of a dress made out of 100 percent hot pink spandex.

When Kevin met me at Arizona State University, I was wearing a salmon-colored mesh tank-style minidress with white cowboy boots and big white hoop earrings. Obviously, that look worked for Kevin.

Driving home from the mall, I anticipated my first date with Kevin and I imagined myself in my new purchase: a rust-colored minidress paired with brown go-go boots, gold hoop earrings, and bangles. Madonna's *Like a Prayer* provided the soundtrack. What a perfect fall-colored palette to wear tonight, I thought. I looked at the clock and it was already 5:17 p.m. I would be ready just in time for an eight o'clock pickup, since I was starting from scratch—that meant washing my hair and conditioning it with Vidal Sassoon hot oil treatment, blow-drying it, setting it with hot rollers, and putting enough Sebastian Shaper hair spray in it to do significant damage to the ozone layer.

I feared the moment Kevin would meet my parents because of my dad's temper. More often than not, my dad flew off the handle because of a simple miscommunication. My parents had a few poorly matched ailments. My dad couldn't hear and my mom only had one vocal cord. Dad, a former Marine, lost his hearing in one ear during combat. He refused to get a hearing aid because of vanity and the related fear of looking old. And once, when my mom was screaming at one of her five kids for making a mess, "right after the goddamn maid had just left," one of her vocal chords suddenly became paralyzed. So she can be heard, but she has trouble yelling or really projecting her yell.

What usually happened was my dad misunderstood my mom and thought she had said something other than what she actually said. Whatever he thought she said would piss him off and then he'd start to yell. We would try to correct the situation by saying, "But Dad, wait, that's not what she said!" He would yell back, "Don't interrupt! Let me finish my goddamn sentence." Afterward, we suffered through an agonizing ten minutes of his ranting.

For example, my mom might say, "Please pass the bread." And my dad would respond, "Fred? You're still dealing with that asshole? I told you to dump him as a client. He's never going to buy a house and we don't need his business. He's a patronizing little fuck with his goddamn Jaguar and the way he pronounces it 'Jag-u-r.'" My mom would try to interject, "But Bob, wait . . ." That only made my dad more angry. "Don't tell me to wait. I've been in the corporate business for twenty-five years. I thought we were partners in real estate. If you don't want my opinion, you can take my name off the twenty-five bus benches now and it will just read 'Pam McDonald welcomes you to Woodland Hills.'" At this point, my mom and I would fight back laughter as she struggled to get the words out. But in no way could she reach his level of volume, causing him to be even more irate.

Before Kevin arrived, I remembered one time when my sister Kathi was waiting for her date, a concrete salesman, to pick her up. Some argument began to escalate to the point where my dad raged about everything and anything. He was mad that he was just hearing (if you can technically call it that) that Kathi was going on a date that night. My mom, in contrast, was happy that Kathi's date sold concrete for a living and was not a roadie for Poison or a Rick James celebrity impersonator. She managed to screech, "But Bob, this guy is into concrete." My dad got even louder and said, "I'm supposed to be impressed that he's into Kathi's feet. What a sick fuck. Just because he's the first guy whose eyes won't be glued to her boobs, we're supposed to jump for joy like a bunch of assholes? Well, unless he's a podiatrist, he's a pervert and he's not going out with my daughter."

About five minutes later, my sister's private line in her bedroom rang and she picked it up. When she returned, she told us it was the concrete salesman and that he was on the walkway when he heard Dad screaming about him and his foot fetish, so he decided it was best he didn't ring the bell. She told him everything was fine and to come back, which he did. My dad felt terrible and actually was impressed that the guy sold concrete. He made conversation and asked where he was from and what college he went to. When the concrete salesman said the University of Michigan, my dad immediately brought up their mascot and said, "Oh you're a Wolverine, are ya?" He then talked sports for a few uncomfortable minutes. Though my dad's outburst didn't help the date, he couldn't be entirely blamed. My sister did admit to yawning several times at Red Lobster when he explained the intricacies of a concrete convention, and they never went out again.

But my dad wasn't a bit embarrassed. He never altered his mood, activity, or volume for anything. It didn't occur to him that I was having eight friends over for a slumber party and that might be the day to forgo his usual routine of swimming naked in our pool except for a pair of goggles and flippers. His daily routine included twenty-five laps of free style with flip turns and ten of the butterfly stroke. No, he never worried that one if not all of my eight friends from the fifth grade might at one point look out the living room window and witness him.

Luckily for me, the night Kevin came, everyone was calm and the meet-and-greet was quick and painless. My parents trusted me and it was understood that I'd be back around one a.m. or so. One good thing about being the youngest of five kids is that by the time you're a young adult, the parents are too old and exhausted to bother to check up on you. With my older brothers and sisters, I'd often wake up to the sound of my parents having been up all night because someone never made it home. They were calling hospitals only to have one of their children walk in at eight a.m. claiming to have fallen asleep at a friend's house while listening to an eight-track tape. When my turn came, they simply took two Tylenol PMs, said an "Our Father," and called it a night.

I decided to take Kevin to a happening bar in our neighborhood called Patty's. It was an English bar with drink specials like Sex on the Beach and Long Island Iced Tea. Kevin ordered a Guinness (he was obviously taking the Irish thing pretty seriously) and I had a Kahlúa and cream. This was long before I knew the caloric dangers of sweet, creamy alcohol. The bar also offered karaoke, and for a brief moment I considered performing my tried and true "Let's Give Them Something to Talk About" by Bonnie Raitt. I can do the raspy voice and had memorized it years before. I never even have to glance at the screen with the highlighted words but occasionally would, just so it wasn't obvious that I practice regularly at home—but instead I chose to lean in for our first kiss. We started to make out at the bar before our second round. I've always been a strong advocate of PDAs. I feel it is only inappropriate when you're sober and witnessing it. When you are partaking in a PDA, it's just two people who are really enjoying each other's tongues. We even made out walking to the car. We made out on top of the car. We made out in the car. We made out underneath the car. . . . Because all I really did was kiss, I believe I was quite good at it and very passionate, too. I was willing to kiss a lot. I would have been a perfect contestant on Brett Michaels's *Rock of Love*.

While sitting in the passenger seat, I'd managed to puff out my chest and arch my back, flipping my long hair from one side to the other. Kevin was saying everything I loved to hear including my particular faves: "You're so hot. . . . You're so sexy. . . . You're better looking than Cindy Crawford." And then he said something that shocked me: "Let's go to your room at USC."

I was totally floored. What? Was my dad's hearing problem in fact hereditary? He didn't just suggest we go back to my room at college?

"Let's go to your room at USC so we can really do this."

Oh my God. This was our first date. Earlier in the evening, I had mentioned that I lived in a defunct sorority house now renamed the Honor House for any members of sororities and fraternities who had a 3.0 grade-point average. I much preferred to live there than in the dorms where my roommate freshman year was a former member of the Israeli army, six-two, roughly 220 pounds, and played the cello. Between her body mass and that of her cello, I barely had room to raise my arms to tease my hair. What had stuck in his mind from the story was the fact that I could go to the Honor House anytime, even when school was on break.

Living with guys and girls in such close proximity made for a lot of fun. During Greek Week, I drank a lot during the day and passed out on my bed with the door wide open. When I awoke, one of the guys down the hall had put a squirt of white lotion on my inner thigh in an attempt to make me believe that a guy came on my leg while I was unconscious. Having never seen cum, I didn't get it, at first, but when I did, oh the hilarity of frat humor. But did Kevin think I was hinting at something when I told him about my college boarding situation?

I immediately pushed his hands off my well-moisturized, Calvin Klein Obsession–scented cleavage and said with an annoyed tone, "Are you kidding me? Did you really think that I was going to have sex with you tonight? Did you think I'd be so desperate to have it that I'd let you drive me all the way back to USC to go do it on my twin bed? How would that even be feasible? You'd have to drive me all the way back to Woodland Hills before the sun came up and my parents awoke. Do you even have that much gasoline?"

Come to think of it, I may also have told him how my dad snores and my mom wears earplugs and therefore they can never hear me when I come home late at night. I guess he interpreted that comment as a major hint that I wanted to have sex all night until the *Daily News* hit our driveway. Was Kevin one of these guys who takes everything you say and do as a major indicator that you want to have sex with them? You could say, "I'm tired."

And then that certain type of guy interprets it as, "Oh yeah. She wants to go to bed with me." You could say, "I want a sucker." And he thinks: "She'd like to suck on my cock like a lollipop." Or you could say, "Look, I'm fucking someone else." And that certain guy interprets it as "Poor guy. She's thinking about me while she's with him."

I asked myself, "Can't a girl dress like a hooker, dance like a stripper, and kiss like a porn star and still be a nineteen-year-old virgin? Why is this such an enigma?"

"I think you should just take me back to my parents' house," I told Kevin firmly as I put on my seat belt and looked straight ahead.

"I'm sorry. I didn't mean to offend you, Heather. I'm just really attracted to you and I didn't mean anything by it."

Well, of course, I forgave him in about three to four minutes. I really liked him and I wasn't going to blow him off for wanting to sleep with me. But at that point I wasn't ready to tell him I was a virgin, either. It was only our first date, and I was fine if he assumed I wasn't one. At my age, not many girls still were. We kissed again at my parents' front door. Kevin said he'd call me the next day, and he did.

Over the next few months, we'd talk on the phone all the time, especially late at night when we'd both come back to our rooms after being out drinking at our respective sorority/ fraternity parties. During one of these intoxicated phone calls, I insinuated that he should invite me to his fraternity's spring formal. I was surprised that he hadn't brought it up yet. That's when he told me that he really wasn't an ATO. He had pledged, but then something happened and he depledged. He said he was still friends with the guys and that's why he was at the party, but he was not an active member. I was in utter shock. Everything I had imagined for us was gone. It was like finding out that Santa is just a creepy fat guy at the mall who gets paid by the hour. No ATO formals were in my imminent future. And this wasn't even the first time something like this happened to me.

In high school, Doug Malcolm was my only kind-of boyfriend. I kept waiting for him to ask me to the homecoming dance, so finally I brought it up with only a week left for me to purchase the iridescent lavender strapless dress with matching silk pumps I'd been eyeing at Macy's. That's when he told me that he had been grounded for driving his dad's car without a license. Sure, the parents wanted to teach their child a lesson, but what about the crime of leaving a desperate fifteen-year-old dateless on homecoming?

I'm sorry, but this Greek thing was my life. It was in my bloodline. To have him tell me he was a GDI (goddamn Independent) was not a turn-on. This was my identity. I was a Gamma Phi Beta and I thought that my long-distance boyfriend was an ATO, but now he was just a junior at Arizona State University—a place where kids went when they couldn't get into USC or any of the University of California schools. If Kevin wasn't in a fraternity, I had no hope of ever getting pinned.

In case you don't come from this world, being pinned is when your fraternity boyfriend gives you his pin in a ceremony on a Monday night in front of all your sorority sisters and all his fraternity brothers. Then everyone gets drunk and hooks up with one another. If the sorority sister getting pinned was dating a guy in a top house, every girl would be dressed to the nines and willing to drop a class if she had a test the next day. If the sister getting pinned was dating a guy in an average to below average house, then suddenly many girls would have to get a two-month jump on finals. Yes, shallow and horrible, but it was my reality at the time. If I was to stay with Kevin, I would never have that fraternity pin, and that was something I had dreamed would happen at college.

Sometimes the calls with Kevin turned sexual but only on his part. He talked about how when he went down on a girl his rather prominent nose was worth its weight in gold. I really was too embarrassed to say anything back or do anything to myself, but I did enjoy listening to how turned on he was. I'd kind of cringe under the covers as we whispered to each other for hours. One night he even told me that he had had an affair with a twenty-six-year-old Playboy Playmate. I immediately questioned how he knew she was in fact a Playmate.

"Did you ever see her spread in the magazine?" I probed.

"No, but her license plate read BUNNY87." Guys will believe anything that will make them feel better about themselves. Something tells me a real Playmate wouldn't want everyone on the 405 freeway and in the grocery store parking lot to know she posed naked in a magazine. "Excuse me, Miss. Sorry to follow you to your car, but didn't I see you on page thirty-eight of the June '87 issue lying on a gravel driveway in nothing but a chauffeur's hat and white gloves?"

That's around the time that Kevin told me our sex life was,

in fact, a carcinogen. I can't help but wonder if Lance Armstrong was severely blue balled at some point in his young life.

Kevin was home in Pasadena for the summer, so we saw each other as much as we could. Still, we were a good hour and a half apart depending on traffic. Sometimes he'd come to the Valley; sometimes I went there. My friends at USC who were from Pasadena performed a clothing style intervention, so I had started wearing things with sleeves and collars. I traded my cowboy boots for flats in an attempt to fit in better with Kevin's town and family. I was becoming a preppy just like James Spader in *Pretty in Pink.*

One thing that bugged me about Kevin was that he was such a snob about the Valley. The night before his sister's wedding, where I was to be his date, my sister Shannon and I went to an all-you-can-eat sushi place. I don't know if it's a cross between inherent frugalness or gluttony or a combination of both, but I now know I can't handle any restaurant with "All You Can Eat" in its headline. I just kept ordering and ordering ahi, eel, yellowtail, octopus, scallops, crab, and imitation crab. It never occurred to me that the fish they were so willing to offer for a fixed price of $19.95 may not have been the freshest catch. That night I puked until the morning. I still felt ill when I called Kevin. I said, "Kevin, I've been sick all night. I think I might be OK by five o'clock for the ceremony, but I just wanted to let you know in case I'm not up to it."

He said, "Do you think your stomach is upset because you're nervous about the wedding and meeting everyone at our country club?"

After ten and a half hours of using the porcelain toilet bowl as my pillow and barely any sleep, I lost it. "No, I ate twelve pounds of bad sushi. I have food poisoning. Look, Kevin, let's get something clear here. You're not a Rockefeller and I'm not Betty from the Bronx. My parents are college graduates who run a successful real estate business. We have a beautiful home which is not in a track area, might I add. Yes, it gets hot here, but last I checked, Pasadena is only ten degrees cooler than Woodland Hills, and we have central air and a huge in-ground recently remodeled pool. Your parents live on two acres and have five kids, too, but still refused to ever build a pool. That's practically child abuse!" I yelled. Kevin apologized, and I felt empowered.

I managed to get myself together and we went to the wedding, where many of the older guests made comments like, "Are you two next?" I knew I wasn't into Kevin anymore when that question made me feel sicker than the sushi from the night before. Later during the reception, Kevin took me into some empty alley and said something about wanting to do me like Andrew McCarthy did Jami Gertz during the family Christmas party in the movie *Less Than Zero*. Now, I loved that movie. But instead of getting me hot, it made me wonder, Do people actually wear thigh-high nylons? In the sex scene, Jami Gertz is still wearing her black nylons, skirt, and pumps. In real life, if you had to wear nylons for an important event, would you forgo the slimming bonus of control-top pantyhose for the bulkiness of that contraption with the clips to hold up the thigh highs just so you could have sex in an alley while fully clothed? It didn't seem worth it.

About a week later, Kevin called me and said he talked to a tarot card reader at a party he went to with his parents. He said, "I asked her about you and she said you were really nervous about losing your virginity and that I just had to be patient and soon it would happen."

This is why I don't believe in psychics now or then. I had no intention of ever losing it to him, and poor Kevin thought it was just around the corner. At that point, I didn't have a physical desire to have sex with him and I didn't want the relationship to get more intense than it already was. I liked having a long-distance boyfriend who I just made out with.

For my twentieth birthday, he presented me with a framed poster of a famous black-and-white photograph of a man and woman embracing at a train station with a handwritten poem that said something about, "How we are far apart, I can sing like a lark." I was flattered that he brought up my singing, because besides my parents and me, no one thinks my voice is that great. I thanked him for it. But the truth was it gave me a stomachache and I never hung it up for display.

Then an explosion happened. Kevin said to me, "I think I'm going to transfer to USC for my final year." Oh God, no. I'm not solely the reason, I thought. USC is a better school for an under-graduate degree, but he made it clear he wanted to continue our relationship once he arrived.

I felt panicked. I didn't want Kevin as a full-time boyfriend. I couldn't date him and still go to other fraternity parties like I had been doing this whole time. I loved dancing at fraternity parties, especially to MC Hammer's "Too Legit to Quit." Those three minutes and twenty-three seconds were sheer hip-hop delight. I'd do the hand move that went along with the song, two fingers up, then make the shape of an L (symbolizing legit), then two fingers up again, then the quit sign across the neck. Then I do my MC Hammer legs going to the left then to the right, next the sprinkler, the chainsaw, and finally the all-sacred running man. A boyfriend would totally suffocate my expressive dance floor moves and I wasn't about to give it all up. Yes, I was shallow—most sorority girls are.

For example, a couple of girls on campus had claimed that they were date raped, each by a different guy but all members of the same fraternity, Kappa Delta. We discussed it at our chapter meeting along with the fact that it was likely that their fraternity would be suspended and thrown off the row.

One of the girls, Marci, piped up, "How do we know they really date raped them?" Another sister argued, "Because it's three different girls all from different sororities all with similar stories."

"Yes, but the Kappa Delts have the best parties and I've already bought my flapper dress for the Great Gatsby Ball," she whined.

I felt my inner Gloria Steinem come out, and I stood up and said, "Look, I know this is not Cal–Berkeley and we choose to shave our armpits regularly. But don't we have enough feminism in our bones to back other women's claims over attending a 1920s party, a theme, which by the way, has been done to death!" I stated this as the majority of the girls cheered in agreement. Besides, the party was a week away and the one

Kappa Delt in my medieval civilization class who I thought was going to ask me was already going with a Pi Phi, so screw those rapists.

I tried to talk Kevin out of transferring to USC. "Really, won't it take you longer than one year to finish and graduate if you transfer?" I asked.

"Yes, but you still have two years left, so it will be fun," he said with a smile.

It was pretty much after that conversation that I started being brief with him on the phone and not calling him back. Clearly, I was afraid of intimacy—both physically and emotionally. What was wrong with me? This guy actually liked my singing voice! He shouldn't be so easily dismissed. But timing is everything, and this was not the time. It was still party time.

I was a junior living in our sorority house. When I wouldn't return his calls on my private line in my room, he'd call on the house main line and ask whoever answered for me. They would come find me, but it got to the point where I'd say, "Tell him that I just left." Then one night at around eight, I was in my room with my roommate and I heard on the loudspeaker, "Heather McDonald, you have a guest downstairs, Heather McDonald you have a guest downstairs!" Oh shit. I literally hid under the covers. I wouldn't go down. I asked my friend Suzanne to go down and tell him that I was asleep. She went and didn't come back for twenty minutes. When she returned, she said, "Oh my God, Heather. Just be honest with him. He was relentless. I told him you were asleep and he begged me to go wake you up, saying that if you knew it was him, you'd want to talk to him. He kept on saying I was a convincing-type person and I could get you to come down. Finally, I said, 'Look, Heather is a total bitch, especially if you wake her up, and I'm not doing it.'" I apologized to Suzanne for making her do my dirty work.

Although I didn't see him that night, I called him and stuck to my story of falling asleep extremely early the night before. We made plans to meet. He was already enrolled at USC, and that night I told him the very original line, "Kevin, I just want to be friends." He said OK, but later that night when he was driving me back to my sorority house, he pulled the car over and walked around to my side, opened my car door, and knelt down and pleaded with me. I didn't know what to say. He started to cry. I remember seeing his giant tear fall onto my light blue jean miniskirt and thinking, God, this guy really likes me. Imagine if he had gotten some actual pussy. What would he be like then? Then I realized he probably did put me on such a pedestal because I hadn't slept with him or anyone else.

Months later, my mom confessed that shortly after our official breakup, Kevin had showed up at our house. My mom was expecting a refrigerator repairman, so when the doorbell rang, she opened it and said, "Oh hi, come in, it's right here. I love my Sub-Zero, but for some reason it's not making ice cubes."

Kevin said, "I'm sorry to hear that about your refrigerator, Mrs. McDonald, but I'm just so sad about Heather."

As my mom told me the story, she laughed. "Heather, I felt so embarrassed that I didn't recognize him right away. But these Sub-Zero guys are so hard to get to come over because a Sub-Zero is like no other refrigerator and you have to have a Sub-Zero specialist fix it; otherwise, they could really fuck it up and . . ."

"Mom," I yelled. "Tell me about Kevin—and how could you have not told me sooner?"

"Well, he made Bob and I swear we wouldn't say anything."

"Dad, you were here and didn't tell me, either?" I questioned.

"Well, I walked in and I thought, Why is the Sub-Zero guy crying and pouring his heart out to Pam? How much is it going to cost to fix this refrigerator?"

"How could both of you not recognize him? You met him like on five different occasions, two of which were full meals." They obviously didn't think he was the one; otherwise, I think they would have paid more attention.

"Well, Heather, you don't know what we had been through with this Sub-Zero. It was five thousand dollars and we hadn't had ice cubes for three days," my mom said.

"Mom, enough with the fridge. What did he say?"

"Well, he was just heartbroken, and I said to him, 'You're a nice, tall guy. You'll find someone else.' And he said, 'Why bother when I already found the greatest girl and she was a virgin,'" my mother explained.

I thought, Ugh, gross, why is he telling that to my parents? Well, of course, the virgin statement made both my parents' afternoon even though the actual Sub-Zero guy failed to show up that day.

One afternoon I went into my dad's Trans Am looking for

a book I thought I had left in there and as I searched under the seat I found something I had never seen before. It was wrapped like a candy. I brought it into the house and opened it. It was round and slimy and looked like a balloon. I said to my mom, "What is this?" And just as I asked the question I realized it was a condom. "Ew, disgusting," I screamed. We soon put two and two together that it was my brother Jim's—he had borrowed my dad's muscle car the night before—and everyone had a good laugh about it, especially my parents, which I felt was so hypocritical.

From the time I started stripping off my diaper and wearing my mom's high heels around the house, she told my two sisters and me that we "must" remain virgins until we were married. She herself was such a virgin that two weeks after her wedding night, she had to have her hymen surgically removed by a doctor. She and my dad had honeymooned in the Bermuda Triangle, but my mom's hymen didn't disappear. Yet when it's her son who is having the premarital sex, it's funny and cool and completely OK? What a double standard. Yes, she should be happy that he was smart enough to be using condoms, but if only for the sake of her daughters, she should have pretended to be just a little mortified at my brother's behavior. Wasn't it a sin for him, or is it only a sin for the woman?

"Look, Heather, you did the right thing, and Kevin did have rather narrow shoulders for his stature," my mom added for good measure.

"He never looked me in the eye the whole time he was crying to your mother. What am I, a potted plant, just sitting there like an asshole sprouting leaves?" My dad has always been quite sensitive and requires a lot of attention.

"Well, I'm glad you finally told me," I said. How weird if my ex-boyfriend would have had a pinky-swear-secret with my parents, who still associate him with the Sub-Zero man who never showed up.

It made me feel bad, but at the same time the whole Kevin experience gave me a lot of confidence. He was really my first boyfriend, and I knew I was capable of being loved by a man without having to have sex with him. So now I could just continue on with my life until I found a guy who I wanted to be my boyfriend and could still enjoy being the blue ballee as much as I enjoyed being the blue baller.

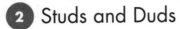# 2 Studs and Duds

The summer before my senior year at USC, I lived at my parents' house in Woodland Hills. I helped them with their real estate business as I had the three previous summers. After I turned eighteen, I got my real estate license so that I could hold open houses and show property. This was a major improvement over the summers during high school when my real estate responsibilities included manual labor. My parents had more than forty bus benches up and down Ventura Boulevard and throughout the West San Fernando Valley prominently featuring both their faces. The ads said: "Bob and Pam McDonald of Country Club Realtors Welcome You to Woodland Hills." The bus benches cost quite a bit of money each month, and one hot summer afternoon my dad decided if the bus bench company wasn't going to clean the dirt and graffiti on them, then my sister and I would.

My sister Shannon and I were scared of my dad and to this day we have never talked back. Our summer days were usually spent stuffing envelopes for their big mailings. Besides the occasional paper cut and dehydration caused from licking envelopes, it was pretty pleasant as we sat in an air-conditioned house watching *The Young and the Restless*. Then my dad said, "The bus benches are a wreck! Take a bucket of water, sponges, and rags and wash them down." He handed us a map of the Valley with red Xs marking each of the benches. Shannon and I obediently gathered up our cleaning supplies, placed them in her car, and whispered to each other, "Is he serious? This is going to suck!"

Our entire livelihood and college tuitions depended on how many houses my parents sold each year. So if dad felt this was necessary, we did as we were told. He even seemed fine about putting us in harm's way for the sake of this business. One time he had us pass out goody bags to all the neighbors that included little refrigerator magnets in the shape of houses, pens bearing their names and number, and scratch pads with their faces, so there were more than fifty pages of opportunity to draw glasses and mustaches on my parents. My dad insisted that we not just drop the goody bag off at the mailbox, because that's lazy, and Bob and Pam go the extra mile—well, they don't, but their kids do—and by mile I mean mile-long driveways up hills to drop this crap off at the doorstep. Sometimes the owner would come out and we'd have to say, "Oh hello. Here is a goody bag with information about the current real estate market and household gifts compliments of Bob and Pam!"

Our primary fear—way greater than the unfriendly owners we encountered—was vicious dogs. When we first started handing these bags out, we were able to get our friends to do it with us and my dad paid them by the hour. After a few days, everyone had quit, the initial excitement of making money in real estate had worn off, and my upper-middle-class friends didn't need the money that bad. But Shannon and I still had eleven hundred bags left to deliver.

I don't blame my friends for quitting, especially after we all witnessed my friend Liz screaming at the top of her lungs, "Dogs, dogs! Save yourself!" while running for her life down a steep driveway as two Doberman pinschers chased her, barking incessantly. Liz ran so fast she fell with all the goody bags. Pens popped open with their springs exposed as the ink stained her along with her own blood. Shannon and I wiped Liz's blood off the pens and put them back together to use in another goody bag. Hey, they were twenty-five cents a pen. Luckily, people don't sue like they do today, and Liz has a nice scar to remember her last day in the real estate business.

I know you're probably thinking, why didn't they just get some Mexicans. But my parents' philosophy was why go Mexican when you can go offspring.

So there Shannon and I were on the corner of Winnetka and Ventura Boulevard with our buckets and sponges ready to wash some commercial bus benches. First, we had to ask the people waiting for the bus to please get up so that we could wash the "Fuck You" off our mother's face. They were confused about what was happening, but I didn't have time to explain how marketing worked by blanketing an area with the same message. As Shannon and I started to squirt the 409 and industrial cleansers, we were whistled at by a bunch of day workers in the back of a pickup truck. "Hey mamacita," they yelled while licking their lips, wetting their fingers, then wiping down their mustaches. "Why don't you wash my dickita next?"

I could tell the people now standing for the bus felt sorry for us but were also relieved when the bus eventually arrived. I had to admit the bus bench appeared more professional, and now it looked more like "uck Y" on my mom's face. The next bench was farther down the boulevard and really needed our help, since it had my dad saying in a drawn bubble, "I sell cock." It was done in permanent marker. After scrubbing for fifteen minutes in the 104-degree Valley heat, constantly wiping away the sweat dripping down from my forehead, I began contemplating if we should just attempt to make "cock" look like "condos." It would read "I sell condos," which they sometimes did, so it would be truthful advertising. Then a carload of Crespi boys stopped at the red light across from us. We went to an all-girl Catholic high school and Crespi was our brother school.

"Oh my God, Shannon. It's a carload of Crespi Critters" (their nickname). "Shannon, duck! Get down!" I screamed as if it was a drive-by in Compton. The light changed, and as they made their left turn, passing us, I heard squeals and laughter. "Nice ass and bus bench," one of them yelled.

"This is awful. Those guys are on the football team. They're going to tell everyone!" Shannon said as she got up, dusted off her knees, and tended to the graffiti again.

"Don't worry, Shannon. They don't even know us," I assured her.

Just then I felt a splash of wetness hit my face and bubbles enter my nostrils as I realized the car had come back around and the boys were spraying us with shaken-up cans of 7UP. One of them screamed, "Hey McDonald whores, is it true over one billion have been served?" And then they sped away. Having McDonald as a last name was not one of the joys of growing up.

In grammar school, my mom told me to tell the teasers that our dad owned McDonald's, which worked beautifully and made me popular for about a week until a smart-ass kid started talking about franchising and how it's not possible to own all the McDonald's. At that point of utter humiliation, we decided to gather up our janitorial supplies with a staggering thirty-eight more bus benches left and simply drive home. Shannon, who was always more sensitive than me, began crying. This really helped our cause when I explained to my dad what had happened and that it simply wasn't safe for us to be out there, besides being unfair to the people who actually use the rapid transit system. For once, my dad admitted he was wrong and never asked us to do it again. (Actually, once there was a shooting and my parents' bus bench was shown on the local news stations several times with the blood spatter on it. My mom said it was the best free advertising they ever got.)

At twenty-one, I enjoyed getting dressed up and showing nice houses. My parents put my face in their ads promoting their properties. My mom received calls asking specifically for me and she loved it. I remember hearing her on the phone: "Yes, she is gorgeous. Well, she's my daughter. Ha, ha. You know, I was Badger Beauty at the University of Wisconsin. Yes, Gena Rowlands was one a few years before me, except that I was the only woman in the history of the university to be a Badger Beauty and military ball queen in the same year. Ha, ha. Well, you should see Heather in person. She's tall and willowy. . . . Of course, she can wear a skirt to the showing. Do you prefer hair worn up or down? Great. She'll meet you at the house—it's more of a mansion really—at three p.m. today. OK. It was so great speaking to you, Houshang." And only then did my mom hang up the phone.

"Mom, what are you doing? You just completely pimped me out. You sound like Heidi Fleiss on the phone, describing me and insisting I wear a skirt," I said.

"Oh come on. He thought you were beautiful in the *Los Angeles Times* homes section ad, and I'm proud that you came from my loins. Now just go to that vacant house on the top of Mulholland and meet him. He's a Persian Jew, so you know he's got money. The only person who is going to buy that monstrosity with its marble and pillars is a Persian. Why did they add all those little rooms that lead to nowhere? It's just a total abortion."

"Mom, can you please not refer to an abortion as additions that were done without permits? It's really an insult to abortions," I argued.

"You know what I mean. Anyway, if you want your tuition

paid for next year, you better try to sell this house. So bring an offer form and put on some heels. He's a leg man."

At least I had my summer evenings to look forward to. Many were spent in Manhattan Beach, where a lot of my sorority sisters were living for the summer. One night, we were at a dance club called 12th Street. This hot spot rocked, because it was full of volleyball players, and I loved looking out at the sea of tall babeness. The only negative was that the dance floor had these lights that did not mix well with my two porcelain veneers. My girlfriend screamed in horror and told me to shut my mouth. She said it looked like my two teeth on either side of my two front teeth looked black. I always had to remember as I danced to "I Like Big Butts" not to smile with teeth, which was a total challenge, because that song just makes you so happy.

On this particular night, a cute girl approached me and asked, "Would you like to be on a new dating show?" Now, I had always dreamed of being on a show called *Love Connection,* but this show was called *Studs.* It hadn't come out yet. It was described as two guys who were known as the Studs who go on three individual dates with three women. So the women end up going on two dates, one with each guy. Then the guys guess which girl said what about them. In the end, each guy reveals who he liked most before the taping began, and so do the girls. If the guy chooses the girl who also chose him and he had the most correct answers, then they get to go on a free trip together to some place exotic like Baja California. My friends all encouraged me to do it, thinking I'd be so funny on it.

The next day, I called the office of *Studs* and they asked me to come right in. They interviewed me about the kind of guy I was looking for. I said, "He has to be tall, dark, professional, and someone who carries a briefcase." Well, I guess they loved that briefcase line, because I had two dates set up for later in the week and a taping set for the following Monday.

The first date was with a twenty-seven-year-old real estate investor, perfect with my vast knowledge of real estate. His name was David Feld. He called me, and since he had an accent, I asked where he was from, and he said Israel. That meant he was Jewish, and I'm, of course, Catholic, but this was just one date for a Fox TV show. He was funny and sophisticated. He picked me up at my parents' house and was well dressed in a nice suit. He took me to Maple Drive, a restaurant in Beverly Hills.

Studs did not follow us with cameras on our date. We told the producers about it afterward, and they wrote the statements and questions for the live taping. David was total Ricco Suave. He was good-looking, and since he came to the United States when he was twelve, his accent was just strong enough to be sexy. He seemed impressed that I already had my real estate license. David told me that he had had one date already with the other contestant, Jan, and it was fine. But we were given stern instructions from the producers not to talk about our other dates. He walked me to the door and I gave him a big hug, though I really "wanted to mall him." This was a quote I told the producer, and it was used in the live taping of the episode.

My second and final date was with Brad. He was an aspiring actor from Texas who worked as a tour guide for Universal Studios. On the phone, Brad told me to wear a really nice dress because after dinner he was taking me to a very special surprise destination. When he came to pick me up, he was wearing a suit, but the suit was light beige, which seemed to fit his personality quite well. He was "light beige," and that was another quote of mine that was used in the taping. I was wearing an off-the-shoulder black cocktail dress with nylons, black pumps, and pearls when we arrived at a pizza and pasta place in a mini-mall. I felt like such an ass eating my fettuccine Alfredo when a baby in a high chair slinging spaghetti narrowly missed my well-coiffed hair. Brad was beige and boring and so straight-laced. After dinner, which could not have cost more than thirty dollars for the both of us and included "two glasses of white zin" (that was how he described white zinfandel when he took the liberty of ordering it for us, even though I hate white zinfandel because it is too sweet), he took me to the big surprise: the Magic Castle. He said that the only way to get into the exclusive Magic Castle is by invitation, and he used his Universal Studios connections to get us in, so it was free to enter. This annoyed me because I knew the *Studs'* producer gave the guys seventy-five dollars toward each date, so he actually made a profit of roughly forty dollars on me!

I've never been into magic and I had to suffer through several shows of "where did the card go" in a state of ennui. Brad really felt that being a tour guide at Universal Studios was his best chance of running into Spielberg and ending up in one of his films. I tried to joke, saying, "Yes, especially if he sees your amazing acting chops when the tour bus goes by the *Jaws* set and you say to the statue of the man fishing, 'Sir, sir, get out of the water. Sir, sir, something is coming your way, sir.'" He wasn't even impressed that I knew the tour guide script verbatim. Universal Studios happened to be where we took every visiting relative because it was so much closer than Disneyland. In the end, he got a hug at the door, too.

When the producer called the next day for our phone interview, I tried to be nice. I said things like "My parents liked him. He was very polite." But then the producer said, "Click, click. You know what that is Heather?" "No," I answered. "That's people turning off their television sets because you are so freaking boring." I warmed up and started to get more honest and TV-friendly. I added, "I thought I was a good girl, but this guy made me look like Madonna." This was also a quote the host pitched to Brad when he asked him which date might have said what. Brad kept guessing the other two girls, but for any complimentary quotes he'd guess me. I'd have to tell him on national TV with a smile, "No, I said you had a face only a mother could love." I felt terrible.

Meanwhile, during the taping it became more and more clear that Jan, a twenty-eight-year-old nurse with frizzy blonde hair, was in love with David Feld and that they clearly had sex. When the moment came for the Studs to make their choice, David chose me and I chose David. Since he had the most correct answers, we won the trip to Cabo San Lucas. All five of us stood up and shook hands and hugged one another as the credits rolled. Jan came over to me with a tear in her eye and said, "Congratulations." I really felt for her. Being a virgin, I could not even imagine how I would feel if I had sex with someone and he did not pick me. Why didn't he pick Jan? She was a sure thing, but men like challenges, and he'd already conquered her.

David and I went out that night and had one other date where we went back to his house, which Jan had described on the show as "contemporary and as sexy as David." It was pretty nice, a tri-level tucked into the hills to take full advantage of the Studio City views. In his bedroom, he brought me over to the bed, and as I willingly went to sit on it, I sank unexpectedly. It was a water bed! I admit, this took place in the nineties, but water beds were officially out of style circa 1983. In fact, I think they had stopped making them entirely, so who knows where David got this thing from. I tried to get up, but I literally felt like I was drowning and trying to grab a buoy. Not only had he not refilled the water bed in years, so I sank deep enough to feel the wood underneath the water mattress, he had satin sheets, so I slid as I tried to get some balance and get the hell out. No wonder Jan slept with him—she had no choice. I heard the water swoosh every time I moved. How can anyone sleep in a water bed? Anytime you change positions, it's like being on the boat *Orca* just as Jaws bit into it.

After making some jokes, including the demand that I see his birth certificate from Israel proving he was twenty-seven because the bed was so outdated, David said, "Is that all you do—make jokes and not make love?" Now I was officially David Felded out. I laughed it off as I swung my leg over the leather ledge of the bed frame and pulled myself up and off the water mattress. It felt good to be land-ho again. (Did I mention that this bed was made of dark wood and had a mirror as the headboard and all these little compartments for books and condoms, I assume, much like Hugh Hefner's very dated bed in *The Girls Next Door*?)

David called me a few times about our free trip to Cabo. The only way we could cash in on the trip was if we went together. I had no intention of going with David Rico Suave Feld. I was not going to sleep with him, and I didn't feel like fighting him off all weekend just for a few margaritas and a room with cold Mexican tile floors in a three-star hotel. I told him my senior year was starting in a few weeks and there wasn't enough time. After two unreturned calls, I believe David regretted not choosing Nurse Jan.

My episode aired on the Thursday a week before the fall semester at USC began. Summer Thursdays were reserved for Strattons, a bar and grill in Westwood. Even though it was UCLA's neighborhood, everyone from USC who lived in or around LA went there. As I walked past the long line, I knew the bouncer, of course, I heard people say, "Wasn't that girl on *Studs*?" It gave me a rush like no other. I thought, This must be how Julia Roberts felt when she was in *Mystic Pizza* and no one knew who she was, but she was the girl with all the hair who served pizza. That night was magical. With each passing comp Jell-O shot, I told my story of how I got on the show and no, I wasn't dating that cheesy David Feld anymore, and yes, I do think he boned Jan on their date, and so on.

My appearance on *Studs* wasn't always so well received. Sometimes I'd be walking on campus and a random voice would yell out, *"Studs."* When the show got progressively cheesier and a guy I was interested in found out I had been on it, he was so disgusted that he never called me again. But the night the show aired, I went home determined to pursue acting and change my major from communications to drama.

When I looked into changing my major, I found that I'd have to stay another year to complete the courses necessary to graduate. I decided to stick with communications, but every time I saw fellow students wearing a pager, that meant only one thing: they had a talent agent who needed to get hold of them immediately when an audition for a commercial or TV show came up. Even the sound of a pager going off gave me a pit in my stomach because I wasn't really pursuing my dream of performing. So whatever extra credits I had, I used to take courses in improvisation or character study.

All the while, my social life was ruled by the fraternities and sororities of USC. The sororities could be broken down into a pretty stereotypical structure. The Thetas were the wealthiest girls with "old" money from Pasadena. They chose their pledges based on looks and what their dad did or owned in Los Angeles. The Delta Gammas were all blondes from Newport Beach and therefore into anything nautical. The Pi Phis were hot, but they had been kicked off the row for two years for doing something nasty, so they were just making a comeback. The Kappas were fun and pretty, but a couple of them were only a few pounds on this side of looking like Kappa Cows. And the Alpha Phis were mostly from the Valley, like me, but were considered a little slutty.

I chose Gamma Phi because my mom was one. They were

the partiers, the drinkers, and I was much more of a drinker than a slut. But to be perfectly honest, the main reason I chose Gamma Phi Beta was because I wanted to play Dorothy in *The Wizard of Oz*. During my rush week, all the sororities put on different plays. Kappas performed *Cats,* Pi Phis did *Grease,* and Gamma Phi did *The Wizard of Oz.* Gammas changed the story and words so that Dorothy was looking for her home and in the end she found it over the rainbow at Gamma Phi with her sorority sisters. After the performance ended, I commented on how well Dorothy could sing, and the sorority sister said, "I know. But she's a fifth-year senior, so I don't know what we're going to do next year." I immediately said to myself in my Bette Davis voice, I do—she's going to be played by Heather McDonald for the next four years. And so she was.

I loved being Dorothy except when I was verbally abused by a drunk disgruntled rushee we had dumped after skit day. She approached me at a bar one night saying, "How you doing, Dorothy? . . . How's your freaking little dog, Dorothy? . . . You know, you and your bitchy munchkins pretty much ruined my life, Dorothy. . . . You guys all acted like you loved me when you handed me those shortbread cookies, but you're just a cunt in red shoes, Dorothy." I felt terrible and yet flattered that my performance made such an impression on her. Maybe I could be a real actress.

I tried to make the best of it, like when I gave a speech on rape for one of my communications classes. After I delivered the well-researched statistics and legal findings, I wrapped up with, "And now for a monologue from the Broadway play and film starring Farrah Fawcett, *Extremities*." I transformed from anchorwoman to dramatic actress as I crouched down to deliver my lines to what was supposed to be the man who had attempted to rape me. Now the tables had turned, and I had trapped him in my fireplace and I was taunting him. When I finished and wiped my tears away, I faced the shocked expressions on the thirty or so students sitting at their desks.

One guy raised his hand and said, "I think you're in the wrong major." Again, I took that as a compliment.

Once, a fellow communications major gave a speech about how she chose our major. She was Asian with a very heavy accent. Her name was Lemon. (At least, that's what she said. I think it was something like Ling Long Dim Sum, but she made it Lemon for short.) Her speech went like this: "When I first come to University of Southern California, I not always communication major. I chemical engineer major. I study so hard, I cry. Professor yell at me, bring me to board in front of whole class, and say, 'Lemon, why you can't do simple equation, you stupid.' That day, I walk past Tommy Trojan and think, college not fun, Lemon not having good time here. Later that day, I turn on TV. It football game. All USC football player communication major. They seem happy. Have time to play game on Saturday. So now, I, too, communication major. Now I have lot of free time. I live on fourth floor in Deans Hall. We do lots of wild thing like go and eat at Ed Debevics. And last Saturday night, we all go to Medieval Times in Buena Park. We crazy."

I could not believe that someone smart enough to be an engineering major dumped it to be a communications major when she couldn't even communicate. It left such an impression that a few years later I did this exact speech as Lemon for a monologue at The Groundlings theater. They were so politically correct at the time, I had to lie and say I was one-eighth Korean so that they would allow me to do the accent.

Every Friday morning in college, I'd do a solid ten-minute routine at breakfast for my sorority sisters about what went down the night before. Who hooked up with whom, who got shot down, which one of us still hadn't made it home, and who hit on our security guard, Leroy. Everyone was just loving my humor.

So when I was in Cabo for spring break (Cabo at last!), I seized a great opportunity to play a joke I knew everyone would appreciate. At one of the bars in the ladies room there was a sign that had one of those stick figures they use in walk/don't walk signs. But there it was—someone throwing up into a toilet with a big X going through it. I took a picture and then went to Kinko's and had them print color copies. Being a sorority house, it was standard to have a percentage of students who were bulimics. But everyone at the house was taking it *sooo* seriously. For example, one night after I downed about ten Jager shots, I got up to get rid of it in the bathroom when the lights went on. About six girls came running in to have an intervention, yelling things like, "No, don't do it. You're thin enough." They pulled my head out of the toilet by my scrunchie and said, "We love you! We're your sisters." Finally, I managed to look up and say, "Don't you get it? I'm not bulimic. I'm an alcoholic."

At about three in the morning, I tiptoed around and put

these no-puke signs all over our bathrooms. We had quite a few with different stalls, since sixty girls lived there. Once you sat down, you'd see a sign on the stall's door. The following morning, I awoke in pure delight, anticipating how great it would be to go downstairs and take full and sole credit for the hilarious prank. I was more excited than at Friday morning comedic breakdown. As I came down the stairs, instead of laughter, I heard girls saying things like, "It's terrible, how insensitive, who would do such a horrible thing, whoever did this should go to a standards hearing, should we get national involved."

I walked in and asked, "What are you guys talking about?"

"Have you gone to the bathroom yet?"

"No," I said.

"Well, these completely unfunny and cruel signs are everywhere," one of the girls said, holding up one of my signs.

"I can't believe the nerve of some people. I don't get it," I said, and I got my coffee and went back upstairs. It was my first experience bombing. Unlike bombing when doing stand-up on stage, I was the only one who knew I bombed, thank God.

Another time that I bombed with my sorority, it was not necessarily my fault. Besides being social chairperson, I was also head of the bubs at rush. This meant I had the power to ax a girl even if her score given by the other girls was high enough to get in. If I felt a sister was giving a "bub"—meaning she was not cute enough, or cool enough, or fun enough to be in our house—a high score because she was a bleeding heart and felt sorry for her, I was instructed by the rush chairperson that I could give the bub a big giant goose egg. Her score would drop significantly and she wouldn't be asked back the next day. To convince our sisters not to be bleeding hearts, we would say things like, "Do you want to brush your teeth next to her for the next three years?" Or, "Would you set her up with your boyfriend's best friend?" If the answer is no, then you are not doing her a favor by asking her to be in this house. The fraternities could only invite a few sororities each semester to party, so having an attractive pledge class was important. We didn't care about their grades. Yes, I know it's awful, and I'm convinced if I go to hell, God will punish me with an eternal rush week.

When I was a senior, hazing of any kind was no longer allowed. But when I was a freshman pledging Gamma Phi, we were hazed. They put the pledge class in a room with a chocolate sheet cake that covered the entire dining room table. We were then told that our pledge class needed to finish it in an hour if we wanted to be initiated. I was ready to do my part and show my devotion to my future sorority. Besides, I love chocolate cake. I started eating cake, really taking one for the team, while a few of the alleged anorexics panicked and threw some of the cake out a window, saying, "I'm not downing empty carbs and sugar for anyone or anything. I'm not an animal." All I really wanted was some cold 2 percent milk to really get this party started. The active members burst in with the grass-covered cake and said, "Not too smart girls. Now you have to finish these pieces, too."

I went over and picked the grass and dirt off before I planned on eating it when some of the girls started crying and threatened to quit the sorority. The rest of the sisters then told the pledge class it was just a joke and of course no one has ever finished the cake. I swallowed my last bite of grass-garnished cake and truly felt like a really fat asshole with cake all over her face.

So at least in my social chair duties, I wasn't hurting anyone.

I loved being social chairperson, talking to the fraternity social chairs to plan "exchanges," which were essentially big parties. I also planned our house parties, which could never be at our sorority house because alcohol was not allowed. For our last party of my senior year, I came up with a western theme and called it "Most Wanted." I wore black leggings, cowboy boots, a western shirt, and a cowboy hat. A cowboy hat is such a flattering look. I love it because I never have to worry about the top of my hair becoming flat or frizzy. Sometimes I wish I lived in Texas solely because I could get away with wearing a cowboy hat every day. I acted as the sheriff and I got five of the hottest girls in our house to come with me and go up and down the row. We went into the frat houses shooting fake guns, stood on their dinner tables, and I'd say, "I'm the sheriff of this here row, and our most wanted men are . . . ," and then we'd list the names of the girls' dates and hand them the invite. Everyone was talking about how cool it was, and the party was getting a lot of buzz. I had found this great gay party planner in Hollywood who was helping me. He found a ranch and caterer, and we were going to have hay rides, full barbecue, and fun-themed alcoholic drinks. Then he said to me, "There's still a little extra money in the budget, so I got something really cool that you are going to love. Do you want me to tell you or do you want to be surprised?"

"Surprise me," I said.

My date was this babe, Tyler. He was a couple of years older, had graduated from college, and was working as a production assistant on the sitcom *Wings*. I met him one night out with friends, and he was tall, dark, and gorgeous. We had been on a few dates. Although he was extremely stupid, I was so excited to take him as my date. I was very close to asking one of the USC dental students who worked in our sorority kitchen in exchange for free meals to be my date. A few girls had done this and it always ended disastrously with the girl having to take her plate up to her bedroom to avoid eye contact with the soon-to-be dentist who had checked her molars with his tongue the night before.

Everything was going great at the party when the DJ stopped playing and said, "Can we please have Heather McDonald on the dance floor?" I thought something needed my attention, so I rushed over to where two guys who I did not know had cleared the dance floor except for one chair in the middle, which they pushed me down to sit in. Then it happened. The music began and these two guys in their early thirties started to strip. Before I could object, one tied my hands behind my back so that I couldn't escape. Next thing I knew, this greasy, overly tanned guy was rubbing his prickly shaved chest against me. I looked at my mortified sorority sisters as I yelled, "No, stop, stop!" But it kept going until they tore off their pants to reveal only a black G-string. Then one of the smelly guys shoved his dick and balls in my face as he grinded his pelvis. I thought I was going to die.

Finally, one of my friends untied my hands so that I could

run away. I found the gay party planner. "This is the surprise, for me or for you? Not only was that disgusting and humiliating, but this is not my party. I just planned if for my sorority house. This is something you do for a bachelorette party or a fortieth birthday. My sorority house is not paying for this, so you better take it off the final invoice," I fumed. He apologized and did not charge us. I do hope he at least got some action from one or both of the gay strippers, because I didn't get any action that night. Tyler was really turned off and was embarrassed that his date was being double teamed on the dance floor. Not only was I mortified, but so was my sorority. Instead of everyone talking about what a cool themed party it was, they talked about how a couple of thirty-year-old gay strippers took over the dance floor.

I didn't hear from Tyler after that night, and with only few weeks left of college, I set out to win the scamboard. The scamboard was a big board with eight of our names on the top. For every guy who we made out with, we'd put his name under ours. We never used the guy's real name, always his nickname. There was "the TA" (teacher's assistant), "the gym guy," "the mole man" . . . The mole man was a gorgeous model with a mole who barely kissed me. But a kiss counted. When I took him to a party where we took some photos together, he was obsessed with getting the pictures back because he was in love with himself. When I went to his place to drop the photos off, he told me how he had a roommate. He lived in a single with a queen-size futon, so that explained why he didn't try anything more than a kiss. I guess the night of the party his "roommate" was waiting at home, keeping his futon warm.

Sometimes I'd make out with some guy who tried to go farther, and I would say no, as always. The next day, I'd be walking to class and he'd skateboard by and just nod his head as if to say, "What's up?" He didn't wait for an answer, because he put his foot down to give himself another push and kept rolling past. Those were the times when I really thanked my virginity. What if I'd gone all the way with him and all I got was a nod in passing, or worse, what if because I slept with him, he went out of his way to avoid me? In the end, I was crowned the winner of the scamboard, with fourteen guys listed under my name. A few of the girls ended up getting boyfriends and becoming exclusive. That wasn't for me: going out drinking, making out with a guy, and never talking to him again was my forte.

I'll Never Geriatric Date in This Town Again

It was April and we were so excited to go to Trader Vic's, the bar inside of the Beverly Hilton on the corner of Wilshire and Santa Monica Boulevards. I wore a black romper one-piece—a sure-fire show-stopping outfit, especially at $108 to be precise—with a halter that showed plenty of cleavage and shorts that displayed full leg. It was a total Heather delight!

I walked confidently into the bar with my two Gamma Phi Beta sorority sisters, Tara and Stacey. Now that we were officially twenty-one, that initial thrill of flashing fake IDs and getting past the doorman was a thing of the past. We headed straight for the bar, where we ordered these huge tropical drinks that had like six different kinds of booze in them and were garnished with white gardenias. The huge bowls of flowery booze had to be held with two hands and cost about twenty-one dollars. But when you had your dad's credit card to slap down, it was an easy buy!

Now, after one of these concoctions, you're guaranteed to develop the confidence, of, like, a supermodel, say, in Minnesota. How could I not have confidence? My hair was in what I like to call an original pouf. I pulled the top of my hair into a barrette so that it pouffed up and outward, while the length of my hair was curled via action-packed hot rollers. It just touched my nipples.

I have always loved big hair. I thought I had a fat face and the big hair helped balance it all out perfectly until I received a comment from my own usually extremely nice sister Shannon. I had landed the part of Claire in *The Nutcracker* and Shannon was a little pissed because she was a junior and I was just a freshman. Usually freshmen were members of the chorus, but the drama teacher chose me for the highly desired lead. Shannon quipped, "You only got the part because Claire is supposed to be a young girl and you have . . ." Then she puffed out her cheeks and smugly pointed at them.

Seriously, I did have the fattest face in town. At fourteen, if someone were to see me driving and just see my head, they would have thought I weighed 200 pounds. In reality, I had stick-thin legs and tiny ankles. Once a boy at my brother's school told me that when he watched me cheerlead for the junior varsity basketball team, he used to wonder how those scrawny legs could hold up the rest of my body.

Quite honestly, I was not attractive at that age, but I had

no idea of my reality because my mother always told me how beautiful I was. She would look at me and say, "Oh those cheekbones!" And, referring to my unkempt, bushy eyebrows, she said, "You look just like Brooke Shields!"

Strange, with all that positive attention, I never could understand why no boys ever asked me out. It was perplexing.

Fortunately, at twenty-one, tweezers and the universe had equalized my features and I looked pretty darn cute. At Trader Vic's, I noticed *him* standing far across the room. His name was Fred Basford. Fred had a full head of hair and a nice tanned face. He smiled at me and I knew then that he was older—late thirties maybe? Well, at least that's what I convinced myself he was. I was always up for something exciting and new.

Fred Basford was tall, probably about six-three. I'm five-nine, so finding someone tall was always a priority. That's not to say I hadn't dated a number of shorter guys through the years—I considered myself an equal opportunity dater—but I have to admit it's kind of a bummer being with someone who you can't look up to. It's no fun constantly having to slouch and develop self-inflicted scoliosis. It's simply no fun trying to figure out what outfits work with a lower heel. Flats are not always "in" and were certainly not during the mid- to late nineties. With a really tall guy, you always feel petite and a little vulnerable.

I feel the same way about a guy's weight. Yes, I love a smooth six-pack, but he has to be buff, too. So a little bit of thickness while still athletic is the best combo to me, though I doubt there are many men who desire female bodies that include unusually small bone density and stomach cellulite.

There I was, twenty-one, my USC college graduation six weeks away, and I was out at what I considered a hot spot with my cute sorority sisters, talking to Fred, this older, sophisticated guy.

It's hard going to bars in your early twenties because you can never afford to eat at the restaurant. By ten o'clock, you look around the tables with their yummy appetizers of shrimp, dipping sauces, maybe a little ahi tuna, and you realize what it must be like to live in Africa. What I wouldn't do to just dive into a pile of those leftover shrimp or chicken skewers.

That's what is great about having a decent job in your thirties: you can actually sit down and order something at these places. But the irony is that by the time you hit your mid-thirties, you don't care about going to the hottest spot anymore.

By now, the gardenia-flowered, multiliquor drink had flowed into my system and I had had no food except for what I ate at my sorority salad bar at about five that afternoon. As my stomach grumbled, Fred asked me what my name was and what I did for a living. When I told him I was a senior at USC, he got all excited. He had gone to USC, too. He was a Beta, a top fraternity made up mostly of hot surfers from Newport Beach.

Eventually, Fred asked me about tennis. Of course, I lied and said I played all the time and was even on the team in high school, young Martina that I was. The truth was my mom gave my sister and me lessons the summer between third and fourth grades, and it was hardly as if we were Vanessa and Serena Williams whipping our white-beaded braids around. I pretty much sucked at every sport, including tennis. Athletics has never been one of my natural gifts. The only thing I ever enjoyed about phys ed class was being picked last with my gay friend Gary.

Yes, even in the second grade I had gaydar and was a full-blown fag hag. Gary and I were always banished to the outfield during baseball. We sang songs from *Annie* and *Grease,* talked about the latest fashion trends, and agonized over what we were going to wear on free dress day, the one day a month we didn't have to wear uniforms. Just as Gary described the Lacoste shirt he was going to wear, a baseball rolled between us and we didn't even notice it. That is until all the other kids started screaming at us.

Gary didn't know he was gay, but I did and I was his biggest champion. I should have been waving the pride flag for Gary even though I was only in grade school. One afternoon in the fifth grade, my friend told me that Gary had kissed Noni, a public school girl who had just transferred in, behind the janitor's shed. I was disgusted. "This is not right," I screamed. "This is not natural. God did not intend for Gary to kiss girls. Gary is gay!" Gary finally came out after high school, where he was the lead in every musical.

There was no filter when it came to TV and life in general inside the reaches of my home. Because my parents were residential realtors, they unintentionally taught me many stereotypes, both positive and negative. For example, Jewish neighborhoods had the best schools; Persians will try to negotiate even after the deal is done; and gay men make excellent, loyal clients who love to flip houses.

At the end of the night, Fred and I exchanged numbers with a promise that I would play tennis with him at his home. Yes, his home included a real north-by-south legal tennis court—*cha-ching*—in Pacific Palisades. This was exciting. Who knew if he would call, but if he did, I was going.

This was way more interesting than going to the 9-0, a bar at the end of fraternity row. I had been going to 9-0 for the last four years with my fake ID. I'd gone a hundred times, and at least ten of those times involved going back the next afternoon to pick up my credit card that I left behind only to be hit with the distinct stench of stale beer in daylight. The only thing more depressing than that is when you start drinking too early in the day, pass out, and wake up the next morning only to realize you missed your own birthday party. You only turn twenty-three and twenty-six once, you know.

I met Fred on a Saturday night, and by Tuesday, I had not thought much more about him. When I returned to my room in my sorority house after classes that afternoon, I checked my answering machine and sure enough heard his mature voice: "Hi, Heather. This is Fred Basford. I met you at Trader Vic's on Saturday night. Give me a call at my office at 310 . . ."

The book *The Rules,* a bestseller about strict rules to follow in order to get a guy to fall in love with you, had not come out yet. One of the main rules, I later learned, is never call a guy first and take your time calling him back. This way you always seem busy and appear to have your own life. I wish the book had come out earlier; it would have saved me a lot of heartache and embarrassment. Without this knowledge, I immediately dialed his office. After getting through the main receptionist to his private secretary and eventually to him, I knew he was quite the powerful businessman, like Victor Newman of Newman Enterprises on *The Young and the Restless.*

Fred asked me if I didn't mind driving to his place and we would go to dinner from there.

"Of course, I don't mind," I replied just a little too eagerly. *The Rules* say to have him pick you up at your place. But was I really supposed to have this older man pick me up at the Gamma Phi Beta house and have our senile housemother, aka "The Phantom," mistake him for someone's father?

We called our housemother "The Phantom" because she was small and skinny and had broken a hip. Therefore, she could not get up past the first floor. But all of a sudden, she'd just show up around a corner out of nowhere like a ghost. Her broken hip was a major bonus for all the girls because we had strict rules while living in the house, which included no boys and no booze upstairs. Since she couldn't get up there, we always "pre-partied" before our exchanges and formals, and guys found their way up via the fire escape.

Fred gave me directions to his home and told me to get there at six that Friday night.

Now the crucial stuff came into play. What the hell was I going to wear on my date? I wanted to look good but classy. Cowboy boots were for sure.

I went to my friend Nicole's room to see what she could lend me. My sorority sisters and I frequently borrowed one another's clothes. Sometimes I'd get into trouble because I would take things like earrings or a scrunchie hair band without asking. Roommates found their belongings over on my messy side of the room and got pissed off. But it wasn't like I was a kleptomaniac. I just grew up with sisters, and there was an unspoken understanding that it was cool to do this. But with some of my sorority sisters, it was not the least bit OK. In fact, it resulted in a long, uncomfortable handwritten letter taped to our sorority refrigerator stating: "HEATHER MCDONALD, PLEASE READ!"

But this time I asked Nicole's permission. Besides, Nicole had the best clothes and style sense. She was our very own Donna Martin from *90210*. Her dad directed many hit sitcoms and her family actually lived in Beverly Hills. Their mansion was just off Sunset Boulevard and had its own movie theater with a real popcorn maker. She went to my high school in the Valley, but during her junior year her parents moved "over the hill" to a gorgeous house on Roxbury Drive.

This was all so exotic to me. I was forbidden from driving "over the hill" in high school. Anything farther than Universal Studios was completely off limits.

I inadvertently broke this rule one summer night when I was fourteen, and I suffered the consequences. My friend Heather—yes, I had a friend named Heather. We were in fact "The Heathers" and our public-school friend Gretchen used to tell our parents we were going to the movies but instead we would walk up and down Ventura Boulevard. On one of these evenings we found ourselves enjoying catcalls from passing vehicles, eating frozen yogurt testers, and reading magazines from the newsstands until a man yelled at us to buy or leave. We then headed back to the theater, where my sister Shannon was to pick us up and take us home.

As we waited a big black stretch limo pulled up and rolled down its back window and who should pop his head out but Jason Bateman! Yes, *the* Jason Bateman. The brown-haired, much cuter, much funnier friend of Ricky Schroder in *Silver Spoons*. Jason Bateman was so my type. Though Ricky Schroder was the star of *Silver Spoons* and Jason just the sidekick, I preferred Jason; besides, I've never been into blonds. Jason and his nonfamous friends invited us into his limo, so we got in, and since there wasn't enough room for all of us to sit, guess who got to sit on Jason's lap? That's right, me, the virgin.

Jason and I hit it off. We all tried to act cool about the whole *Silver Spoons* fame. Also, Jason was a lot older than us, he was seventeen, so we didn't want to appear immature. As we were laughing I noticed my sister's car pull up behind us. We decided to tell my sister the truth but that we were going to all sleep at my friend Heather's house so we could spend time hanging out with Jason and the limo friends. I hopped off Jason's lap and talked to my sister, and when I returned, who's now sitting on the *Silvers Spoons'* second lead's lap but my other friend, Greedy Gretchen. Bitch.

Our first stop was a diner about ten minutes down the boulevard in Sherman Oaks called Du-par's. There Heather called her mom and told her we were just getting something to eat with my sister Shannon and then Shannon would drive us home. When Heather and I returned to the booth, there was Gretchen all over Jason, feeding him french fries, and laughing.

I was so pissed. She was completely hogging the conversation. I wanted to ask Jason about his sister Justine, who was on *Family Ties*. Did he know the cast and were they concerned that Tina Yothers was no longer cute and that's why they added a baby? I had lots of questions and thanks to Gretchen I had no opportunity to ask them.

When we got back into the limo, I thought we'd start heading back toward the West Valley where we lived but instead we got on the freeway and merged onto the 405! *Oh my God, what is happening?* I thought. My dad had a strict rule that Shannon and I could not go "over the hill"—nothing east of Sherman Oaks. My dad believed our older sister Kathi's wild behavior was a direct result of her going "over the hill" and hanging out with "The Holly Crowd," as he would refer to it. Holly was short for Hollywood and he didn't want Shannon or me ever to be on a first-name basis with the bouncer at the Rainbow on Sunset Boulevard.

"Where are we going?" I questioned, trying to sound cool.

"We're going back to the hotel?" Jason answered nonchalantly.

"What hotel?" I asked, now concerned.

"The Beverly Hills Hotel, that's where we're staying?" Said one of his friends who had a Southern accent. I had no idea his friend was Southern. I'd barely paid any attention to anyone other than Jason and Gretchen.

Next thing I knew we were in a hotel room in the Beverly Hills Hotel watching *Risky Business*. Well, I had seen *Risky Business* at that point about twelve times and Tom Cruise hadn't even done his gay dance in his briefs and Ray-Ban sunglasses yet so I knew there was more than an hour and fifteen minutes left. Heather and I started to freak out it, as it was already one a.m., but we couldn't call her mom or my parents and say, "We lied. We are at the Beverly Hills Hotel and it's a simply stunning room with palm trees wallpaper and Gretchen is off with Jason Bateman." My stomach started to get the pit feeling, which I still get today when I know I'm going to get in trouble. We started to get more and more stressed when the Southern guy said, "This is ridiculous, you girls need to get home, let's have the limo take them back."

In this case a Southern guy proved to be a gentleman. So Heather and I decided to walk around the hotel, hoping to find Gretchen so we could all leave. After looking for about ten minutes, Heather turned to me and said, "Let's leave her. She'll find her way back, she went to public school."

"Are you sure?" I asked, thinking *What would Jesus do? Would Jesus leave his apostle at the Beverly Hills Hotel, if it meant pissing off his mother, Mary? Yes, I believe he would leave his apostle at the Beverly Hills Hotel.*

"Yes, we need to get back. You know that our parents have already talked to each other and already figured out our lies. Our parents don't even know Gretchen's parents' number to call them, so she's got nothing to lose," she argued.

"All right, let's get out of here," I said.

The whole ride home I just kept imagining my dad's burgundy Trans Am in Heather's driveway, and the thought was making me sick. The guys dropped us off and as we walked into Heather's living room, Heather's mom went running to the window to see who had dropped us off. Before we could explain the truth, all my nerves and fears of getting in trouble got to me and I ran to the bathroom and threw up a little, giving Heather's mom the suspicion that we'd been drinking, which we hadn't. We told her the truth and said that Gretchen personally knew them from public school and that they were taking her home. We both ended up getting grounded for two weeks, along with my poor sister for lying for us. However, my mom the star fucker she can be, was really impressed with the whole Jason Bateman aspect of the story. She even had the nerve to ask if he got my number and talked about what a coup it would be if I could take him to a high school dance. Imagine the pictures we could send to all of Bob's relatives back East!

I loved that Nicole lived "over the hill," and she agreed to lend me a very non-Valley outfit.

Nicole gave me a flattering black skirt, just above the knee, way longer than what I was comfortable with, a black tank top, and a very cool fitted cranberry blazer. This was "in" at the time and apparently so was dressing like a corporate slut. Remember *Ally McBeal* and Heather Locklear's short skirts on *Melrose Place* (the first time around)?

We all agreed that this was the perfect look for a twenty-one-year-old college senior to go to dinner with a thirty-eight-year-old (or, so I told myself) real estate mogul.

My roommate Stacey was concerned. "You don't know this guy. He could be a mass murderer," she screeched. This was before the convenience of Googling someone or typing a guy's zip code into a registered pervert site to see if his name popped up. All I knew was location, location, location, and I doubted many murderers lived in the hills where mansions naturally included tennis courts—well, besides Phil Spector, but I would never date someone with hair like that, anyway.

I was definitely nervous but completely intrigued. Every first date is nerve-racking. It's a lot like auditioning for a role. You get as pretty as possible, try to come off relaxed, and hope that they call you back. In fact, one of my friends, Jennifer Coolidge, whom I later met at The Groundlings theater, set me up with her executive producer from a TV show she was on. I was always attracted to what I like to call the "industry Jew." Jewish men who wore little black-rimmed glasses and had a job in Hollywood truly did it for me. I always thought that would be an ideal match for me, the shiksa. This would only work, however, provided he would allow us to raise our children as Catholics.

I met with Jennifer's industry Jew and he was instantly not attracted to me. I could tell this because the whole conversation was him asking me if I knew any funny "guy" writers. At the time, I had already been a staff writer on a network show, which I reminded him of, but he kept asking, "What guys did you write with? Who do you know that's on *Saturday Night Live*?"

After the date, Jennifer called me and said, "Well, I talked to Joel . . ." The rest of what she said was just like what your agent would tell you when he tries to let you down gently that you didn't get a part. "He's going to pass. It's not you. He thought you were great and really funny. It's just not what he's looking for right now. Don't feel bad. There is something better out there for you and we're going to find it. Besides, he dates his assistants, bimbos. I shouldn't have even sent you out on this one. . . . I just thought maybe it could lead to something else."

Driving up to Fred's house, I had the same nervous feeling I would get years later driving through the Paramount lot for yet another sitcom pilot audition. The house, or rather the mansion, was gorgeous. He had told me he scrapped the original house a few years prior and designed and built this one from the bottom up. I drove past it, checked the address a couple of times, and decided to park on the street, not in the circular drive, as I didn't want to block anyone.

My car, a red two-door Celica, was new, and I was such a geek that I even had a personalized license plate that read USC MCD. I felt like "the bomb" at the time. I was early by, like, twenty minutes. I thought about waiting outside, but then I thought, No, have confidence, you're here now, go in. So I walked up to the door, which was massive, and rang the bell. A Latina woman in a full-on maid's uniform opened the door.

"Hi, I'm Heather. I'm here to see Fred," I said oh so politely.

"Oh, yes, Miss Heather. We've been expecting you. Please come in," she said in a subservient Spanish accent.

The interior of the house was equally stunning. There was even a dramatic MGM-like staircase and rich woods, but the house was still light and bright. The maid walked me through the foyer into a less formal living room. "Would you like something to drink?" she asked.

"No, I'm fine, thank you." I learned later in life to always take the drink, whether it is coffee, wine, or water. Why the hell not? It makes the hostess or the receptionist feel much better when she looks at you fifteen minutes later and you're still sitting there doing nothing.

She left and I remained seated on a dark leather couch.

I began to look at a big coffee-table book on fabulous pools by Kelly Klein. See, I thought, I may be twenty-one, but I can read! I'm interested in books and architecture and fancy pools. And I already have my real estate license!

Fred came into the room wearing shorts and—I kid you not—a USC sweatshirt. Yes, I know; I remember you, too, are a Trojan. At this point, I did start to think he was looking more like he was in his forties than the thirty-eight years I had initially estimated.

"You're here early," he said, somewhat taken aback.

Shit. Why didn't I just sit in my car down the street and rock out to En Vogue on the radio?

"I got here quicker than I expected," I replied.

"Really, even with Friday night, traffic?" he questioned.

Yes, Fred, I thought, because, you see, I'm a freak and I left a little after four to get here by six so as not to be late. I am always on time. People are either always on time, fifteen minutes late, or hours late. There is no in-between. I guess I'm always afraid of missing something when I socialize. Everyone knows the seven-layer bean dip is the first thing to be devoured. I also never want to inconvenience someone, and when you're late, you do that.

Fred asked me if I wanted something to drink. This time,

I said, "I'll have vodka with cranberry juice." He called out for Maria and said that he would have the same. First with the sweatshirt and then with the drink? Hmm. I get it. We're so much alike!

Then he introduced me to Maria's husband, who I guess would be considered his butler. The couple lived on the property and helped run it. Mañuel, the husband, was busy making gourmet Wolfgang Puck–style pizzas in the wood-burning oven that Fred had built especially for that purpose. This was to be our appetizer. Next, he asked if I'd like the grand tour.

"Of course, I would," I replied.

Fred took me through each impeccably decorated room. The house must have been about thirteen thousand square feet. He took me into his master bedroom. It had two separate master bathrooms en suite, one for Him and one for Her. The Hers included a big vanity, whirlpool tub, and shower. It was all done very femininely. His bath was rich and stately with dark green granite and chocolate wood cabinetry. What a brilliant design, I thought. Even in lavish baths you still have to share a toilet, but not here.

Fred showed me his closet, and then, with a flourish, "Hers." Now this closet was enormous and empty because he was single and had never been married. It even had a special room inside it specifically for furs in order to keep them at a certain temperature at all times. Fred turned to me and asked, "Do you think you could fill this one day?"

"Maybe," I giggled.

God, could I? Could I just go straight from college to marrying this rich older man and that would be it? I would just shop every day and have expensive dinners out. I'd always be significantly younger and he would always dote on me. How jealous would my sister Kathi, twenty-eight at the time and married with two kids, be? I knew I was mature for my age, because I believed I was mature for my age. But what about all those beer commercials with twenty-five-year-olds drinking and playing volleyball with other twenty-five-year-olds on the beach? Was I ready to kiss all that goodbye for a fur closet? OK, no need to decide at this minute, Heather. Let's just get through dinner.

Fred excused himself to change while I waited. When he came back downstairs, he was dressed nicely in slacks and a long-sleeve button-down shirt. He walked me into the garage, where he decided that we would take the Ferrari to dinner. It was cherry red and there were these long cushions hanging from the ceiling of the garage so that when you opened the doors to the Ferrari, there was no way it would hit the Mercedes or the BMW parked on either side of it. He drove us to Chinois, a Wolfgang Puck restaurant in Venice.

As we valet parked, of course, I could practically hear the snickers coming from the valets. A young girl with a clearly older man—"Gold digger!" I imagined them saying this and much more to each other. I guess my blazer didn't fool them. They must have known it was Guess, not Armani.

At dinner, Fred and I honestly had a great conversation. He was smart and funny, and if he was thirty-something, that was still not even close to my dad's age, who was forty-five when he had me.

After our fabulous dinner, we drove to some Wilshire Corridor high-rise to meet his uncle. Why, I don't know. Maybe he wanted to show me off. Fred told me his last girlfriend was a twenty-seven-year-old model. At the time, I felt that twenty-seven was so much older than me. He said, "I had just had surgery and asked her to make me some soup, but she wanted to go out and buy it. I said I was so disappointed that she wouldn't make it from scratch."

I almost said, "Oh Fred, how simply terrible. How hard is it to open a can and pour it into a pot?" Thank God I stopped myself and realized that some people do make chicken soup from an actual chicken. I thought, note to self: learn how to make soup.

"What surgery did you have?" I asked.

He was hesitant and said that it had to do with something "down there," but assured me that "everything is fine now."

As we rode in the elevator after visiting the uncle, we kind of grabbed each other and started kissing. Making out with Fred was fun. There were only a few flights to ride, so we couldn't go too far.

When we arrived at his house, he didn't ask me to stay or anything like that. He walked me to my car and said he'd call me. When I got back to the sorority house, I stopped at the second floor and told Nicole and a couple of the other girls the whole story with all the details and we ended up talking until about two a.m.

Just then, my roommate Stacey came down from the third floor and screeched, "Heather, you're here. I was so worried about you. I thought you were dead. You go to this weird older guy's house and then never return."

Poor Stacey. She knew I was no slut and that I practically wore the scarlet V for virgin around my neck. So if I'm not out having sex, I must be in a gutter dead somewhere. Most of the girls, however, didn't know I was still a virgin, because at twenty-one, it's embarrassing. I never really talked about it. Besides, if I had told them, they probably wouldn't have believed me. In fact, my sophomore year a rumor went around that I had sex with two guys in the Sigma Alpha Epsilon bathroom! What bullshit. I hadn't even given a blowjob in my life. Apparently, that is what is said about you when you dance on tables in short skirts and cowboy boots.

The next date involved the dreaded tennis, which I had told Fred I was so good at. He told me that we would play tennis, swim, and then have dinner with some of his friends. I said, "Sounds great," but knew I couldn't play tennis for shit. When I got there, Fred was playing with some bald fifty-year-old guy whose girlfriend was thirty and not that hot.

When he suggested we play doubles, I said, "I'm so bummed. I packed my swimsuit but forgot to pack my tennis shoes. I'm wearing sandals."

How brilliant was that? I hate sports dates, biking, hiking, skiing, and Rollerblading. They all suck. It's like an added test. How cool are you? Are you sporty and low-maintenance? Do you love going to baseball games and eating Dodger dogs? No, I don't! In my opinion, the only dates that are acceptable involve drinks and dinner. In fact, the best dates always involve drinks and dinner. I changed into my bikini, which I admit looked pretty good on me. At twenty-one, I could really pull a two-piece off, especially because I had a tan from real UVA rays. And there were no orange self-tanner streaks around my ankles or white handprint on my thigh, like I often get today.

Dinner, which we had at the house, included the bald friend, his snippety girlfriend, Fred's personal trainer, and the trainer's wife. The talk quickly turned to real estate, at which point I announced I had gotten my real estate license two summers ago, but I had a job working as a buyer for a major department store, which would begin in August.

Why didn't I just hand them my college résumé?

I was so determined not to be a loser, to have a good-paying job straight out of college so that I could live on my own and not be thought of as an idiot. I was afraid to go into entertainment then, because growing up in LA, everyone is so jaded about the business.

I didn't want to be a waitress at twenty-eight. I wanted to be financially independent or marry a really rich guy—whichever came first.

The annoying girlfriend questioned me, my age, what I was doing. . . . It was almost as if at thirty she was so much more sophisticated than me.

I actually saw her a year later. She had had the bald man's baby, out of wedlock, of course, and was still hoping he'd marry her. Guys don't have to worry half as much about knocking up

a twenty-one-year-old; it's the women in their thirties and forties who keep getting pregnant "by mistake." After having your
monthly period for more than two decades, shouldn't you know
your cycle by now?

That night, like the previous date, ended pretty innocently,
too. Fred and I just kissed and he walked me to my car. I think
he was really kind of falling for me. Because my parents were in
real estate my whole life, even though I was still young, I could
absolutely keep up and contribute to the conversation. He said
he wanted to throw me a graduation party. No way, I thought.
How awkward. I'm supposed to invite my twenty-one-year-old
friends to my forty-year-old boyfriend's mansion? I knew I
wasn't going to be having sex with him by graduation, but I felt
I would really owe him something if he threw me a big party.
I couldn't invite my parents. What would they think? I guess
they could talk politics and discuss where they all were the day
Kennedy got shot. The whole idea of it made me nervous. So I
just laughed it off and said, "No, that's not necessary."

The following Saturday, we made plans to go to the beach.
We met at his house and drove to his beach club, the Jonathan
Club. I loved the Jonathan Club. Throughout college, whenever
we wanted to go to the beach, I would get on the PA system and
say, "Whoever is an active member of the Jonathan Beach Club,
please come down to the foyer. I would like to drive you to the
beach so we can use your membership number. Jonathan Club
members only, please!"

A beach club makes a trip to the beach so wonderful. There
are the cocktails, guys to put the umbrellas up, clean bathrooms,

and finally attractive people whose bathing suits fit properly. My parents were never members of any beach or country club; with five kids and their busy careers, they didn't have the time or the money.

When we arrived, I wondered if people thought I was Fred's daughter. But since he was a member, they must have known he had no children. Maybe they thought I was his niece, like in the movie *Pretty Woman.* He wore his Beta fraternity sweatshirt! Come on, you're in your forties! As much as I love my sorority house, no one should get a tattoo representing their house or be seen wearing the sorority or fraternity paraphernalia after age twenty-four.

Spring break in Cabo San Lucas was funny because we saw all these locals wearing T-shirts that said things like "Pi Phi" and "Kappa Sig Luau." I guess some drunk Pi Phi or Kappa Sig just left the T-shirts behind a few spring breaks back. We pointed at an old Mexican woman selling silver necklaces, spotted her T-shirt, and said, "Looks like Pi Phi got some older international pledges this year."

As Fred and I settled into our beach chairs, I saw a couple of guys I knew from college. I wondered if they understood I was on a date. Did they think I was a gold digger, too, like the valets? I imagined myself five years from then with two little kids, maybe pregnant with the third. Would Fred be a hands-on dad, or would we have Maria and Mañuel with us in their uniforms chasing the kids around on the sand as I lay passed out drunk in a lounge chair with the other wealthy mothers?

On the fourth date, I met Fred at his house on a Wednesday

at four p.m. and we worked out with his personal trainer in his gym inside the house—yet another physical activity date. At least I would just have to complete the reps I was instructed to do, which doesn't take great athletic ability or balance. I ended up not minding this at all. I would work out more if someone else was paying someone else to make me do it. When it's just me attempting to exercise, I stop at about six reps or two minutes in, whichever comes first. I tell myself, "You don't want to get too muscular and be mistaken for Madonna."

Fred and I then went swimming. His body wasn't bad. Sure, his skin wasn't as taut as a twenty-three-year-old's, but he was no doubt sexy. The bummer was I had to get my hair wet. It's not like I'm a black girl and absolutely cannot get my hair wet, but it's thick and takes time to properly blow out and curl. However, I loved getting ready to go out again in the "Hers" bathroom. I had to rush so as to not appear too high maintenance; I only blew my hair for a few minutes, letting it dry naturally, and came out in jeans and a casual top. Fred complimented me on how fresh I looked. Probably anyone twenty-five years younger than him looked pretty freaking fresh!

We went to a really nice Italian restaurant close to his house. When he called to make a reservation, he picked up the phone and dialed from heart. He said, "Marco . . . I'm great, thanks . . . Yes, tonight; say in about fifteen minutes. I'll be with my friend, Heather." Wow, the maître d' knew who he was just by hearing his voice? This was before caller ID, and I was most certainly impressed.

At dinner, Fred confessed that his friends had been asking him, "What do you talk about to a twenty-one-year-old girl?" He said he told them, "She's very mature, funny, and smart."

What a nice thing to say, I thought, and so true. Just look at me. I had all of this going on. Maybe this could work out? Maybe I could fall in love with this guy. He is attractive and tall and fit and really fun to talk to, and hell, he was even in a good house, Beta. I hit the jackpot. We could go to USC football games together for the rest of our lives. Sure, it would always have to be with his friends and their bitter forty-something-year-old wives or their insecure thirty-five-year-old second wives or their pregnant thirty-year-old girlfriends, but who cares? We'd be in the VIP box with a fabulous parking pass.

When we returned to his house, we went up to his bedroom to watch TV. We snuggled on a lounger and started to kiss. He was a good kisser and I was getting into it. I knew there was no way I was going to have full-blown sex with him. Remember, I was a virgin, but I was ready to have some fun. He maneuvered himself on top of me. I could feel his erection on my jeans. We kissed for about five seconds more when he said to me, "Ah, just hold me."

"What?"

"Just hold me," he somewhat demanded.

So I wrapped my arms around his back and kind of hugged him as my confused face stared up at the crown moldings. I then looked at him and saw his mouth open, his eyes roll back into his head, and he let out a moan.

I had no idea what had just happened, but then all of a sudden he just got off of me and stood up. He reached out his hand and helped me up and then abruptly said, "OK, I'll walk you out."

Whoa. Wait. What had just happened? Then I noticed a perfect circle of wetness on his khakis just to the left of his penis. Oh my God, he just ejaculated, after only one minute of making out! He didn't even touch one of my boobs. My bodysuit was still all snapped, secure, and tucked into my jeans. My belt was still fastened; my boots were still on.

I know I'm hot, but not that hot.

I was in total shock as Fred walked me down the staircase through the front door and to my car. He gave me a quick peck and I got into my car, locked my doors, put on my seat belt, started the engine, and drove off saying to myself, "What the fuck just happened? And where the fuck is the 405? Get me the fuck out of here."

I talked to myself the whole drive home. "Oh, so that's it? He comes and then I'm out, asked to leave like a hooker? Then again, if being a high-class hooker was this easy, it might be worth it."

I was obsessed with street and high-class prostitutes since I was a little girl and saw the made-for-TV movie *Dawn,* starring Eve Plumb, who played Jan on *The Brady Bunch.* Dawn was a teenage hooker in Hollywood and walked the streets in a brown suede minidress.

I was a hooker for Halloween for three years straight from the second through fourth grades. As I put my shiny outfit together and put on a ton of makeup, my mom never bothered to ask me—her eight-year-old daughter—what I was dressed as. One Halloween, I added roller skates to my costume and was a hooker on wheels. I guess so that I could turn more tricks quicker. Of course, I loved hooker outfits. Who doesn't? I loved Jodie Foster in *Taxi Driver.* For a ten-year-old hooker, she really seemed to have her shit together. Either that or girls with raspy voices just come off sounding like they have a better understanding of how the world works.

I've always been fascinated that women could have sex for money. Victoria Principal played a mistress in a TV movie once, too. Her character was an actress who was kept by a wealthy married man. In one scene, she came bouncing out in a bikini to tell him that she'd booked a part in a soap opera that week, to which he replied, "But next week is my business trip to Chicago and that is our only time together."

As a nine-year-old watching this, I yelled at the TV: "Hey asshole! Let her film the part. It's a soap opera. It could lead to her being a regular. Maybe even a daytime Emmy. What kind of monster are you?"

Thankfully, my parents weren't home to hear my tirade. I continued: "Victoria, dump him. You could be on the cover of *Soap Opera Digest.*"

But Victoria's character knew she had to go to Chicago. That was part of the deal, which also included a gorgeous condo with a pool. Later in the movie, the married man died, and since she was just his mistress, he left her nothing in his will. In the end, poor Victoria Principal had to resort to being just another high-class call girl in Beverly Hills in order to sustain her life-style and pay her homeowner fees.

But I was not Victoria Principal in an ABC television movie. I was Heather McDonald, a soon-to-be college graduate.

I thought about my options: What if I continued dating Fred and what just happened became our entire sex life? Forget ever experiencing an orgasm—I may never get to experience sex at all. It will just be him laying on me for one, maybe two minutes while I hug him and then he comes.

Gosh, he didn't even diddle my do. Nothing. But now it all made sense; this is why this total package of a guy was never married and never had any kids. What was the surgery he had when he was with the last girlfriend, the model? Maybe she was hoping some doctor could fix his erectile dysfunction, and until she knew he could sustain an erection for longer than ninety seconds, she wasn't going to bother to learn how to make soup.

Fred called me several times after that night and I never returned his calls. At the time, I didn't tell my friends the awful truth about his pre-ejaculation problem. I just said that it didn't work out between us. He called me again a couple months later and I answered the phone at my parents' house. I must have given him that number at some point. He asked me what happened and he joked, "Did I have bad breath?"

Hardly. More like bad control of sperm.

But instead I said, "No, I just had graduation and had to move and everything."

He invited me to a Fourth of July party on his boat in the marina. Even though I had no plans other than eating hotdogs with my parents, sister, and her kids in our backyard in the Valley, I decided to pass and politely said, "Oh, I would love to, but my boyfriend's family is expecting me."

He answered, "Your boyfriend? Well, lucky guy. Have fun and call me if he ever makes you mad. Ha, ha."

I replied, "Sure will."

Telling a guy who you are no longer interested in that you have a boyfriend or better yet that an old boyfriend and you are going to give it just one more try is the best and easiest way to end it with someone. How can anyone compete with a relationship that has such history? Sometimes I would get so into the made-up ex-boyfriend who is begging for me back story that I almost believed it myself. I would be sad when I hung up the phone and had to face the reality that yes, the guy I'm not into anymore won't ever call me again, but neither will the ex-boyfriend who doesn't exist.

I didn't find out how old Fred really was until after we stopped seeing each other. I was with some friend of my parents and I noticed an old USC yearbook in their bookcase, so I started flipping through it when I saw Fred's face with a bunch of fraternity brothers from the early seventies. Was it entirely possible that Fred had dodged Vietnam? Disgusting! Good thing I was never hired to be an age guesser at an amusement park.

Many years later, I was at the Jonathan Club with my friend Tara when we saw Fred. He was married to a very pretty twenty-five-year-old former flight attendant. Tara, being a member of the club, had given me all the details. Fred was playing with and was completely enthralled by his child, who appeared to be about one. They've since had two more children. Who knows how? Was he able to fix his problem by going to one of those doctors I hear advertised on FM radio, or did they have to do infertility treatments, or are they in fact his personal trainer's children?

Fred's wife did seem completely relaxed as she lounged, thumbing through the latest issue of *Cosmopolitan* magazine and drinking her margarita while Fred and Maria chased after the toddler. Maybe for them this was the perfect life.

On the bright side, Fred introduced me to blended mango margaritas, the most delicious drink ever, and taught me a very valuable dating lesson: if he seems too good to be true, he could be a pre-ejaculator.

4 Phil Roberts

After graduating from USC, I lived with three of my girl-friends in a big ugly pink flamingo-colored apartment building built circa pre-Heather. It had yellowish cottage cheese ceilings and a balcony overlooking a pool that could have carried the West Nile virus. But who cared? At least it was in the heart of Brentwood on the west side of LA. The four of us called it the "pink palace" because to us it was a palace for USC princesses who lived more like pigs with clothes and makeup and take-out containers hanging off ceiling fans.

Right after college graduation I dated a guy I had briefly dated in the fourth grade and therefore believed might just be my soul mate. He knew I was a virgin and on one rainy afternoon in this very apartment when we were all alone I briefly considered losing my virginity to him but quickly changed my mind when in a moment of clarity I realized I personally knew three girls he had devirginized in high school. The first girl was in the backseat of his Mustang, the second on Zuma Beach by lifeguard station 6, and the third girl was on the first girl's bed at her seventeenth birthday party. Despite our history, mostly at roller-skating parties held on Catholic holidays, I could not let him be "the one," out of respect for myself. I could not be #4 on his D-V'd list. So we broke up and I focused on what I thought would be my career.

My first job out of college was as an assistant buyer for the department store Robinsons May, which was eventually bought out by Macy's. I nailed the position because on my way to the on-campus interview, I ran into my friend, who told me every question they asked. I was able to wow them with my prepared answers about how it had always been my life's desire since I first began removing clothes from my Barbie dolls to one day be a buyer of a major department store. "And Robinsons May is the grandest of them all . . ."

When the interviewer asked if I had any more questions, I did the classic interviewing trick and asked, "Yes, I'm so naturally curious. What made you decide to get into human resources? It seems like it would be just so fascinating!" The woman lit up. Sucker! She then told me her whole life story about being a flight attendant (pretty juicy story, and as I continued to ask for more details, I got them), about how she got involved with a married pilot, then took an indefinite medical leave of absence recommended by her psychiatrist. She eventually found herself in a totally new field. As I convinced her that the pilot was still in love with her and she should just continue to fly that airline in the hopes of running into him and accrue frequent flyer miles, I knew the interview could not have gone better and the job was mine.

Within days, I realized the job was not for me. I could never admit it, even when my one friend in our thirty-person training group, Maia, pulled me aside by a stack of sample sweaters and whispered, "What do you think?" I answered with a Stepford wife smile, "It's great." Maia then said, "Are you kidding? This totally sucks. I'm getting my résumé together and breaking out by Christmas."

It did suck. Maia was right. I was stuck in a cubical all day. I was not choosing clothes and deciding in which store they would best sell. I might as well have been a bean counter on a factory assembly line. The most creative it got was when I piped up in a meeting that we should order more petite sizes for a store in a city that I personally knew had a high Philippine population. Even then, the thirty-year-old bitch I worked for took all of the credit. She was single, a little overweight, and completely passive/aggressive.

One day, she turned to me and said in a rather snarky tone, wearing an Ann Taylor Loft reject, "This is hard for me to say, but you might want to rethink the length of your skirt. When I give you something to hand to the executives upstairs, that is the only time they see you. Their only impression of Heather McDonald is a twenty-two-year-old in a very short black skirt and heels. Unfortunately, those executives are all male and they have been talking about you. I thought you might like to know." Thanks, Miss Bitter, for the 411. Of course, I wanted to know this information. What a major turn-on, to think that all the fat older men running the corporate retail offices thought I was this hot slutty thing. It made me feel like I had a leg up on my competition. The last thing I was going to do was start wearing longer skirts to please the bitch whose long shapeless skirt happened to be covered in cat hair every day. Why didn't someone in upper management pull her aside and hand her a freakin' lint brush? This was the one exciting thing that happened on the job in the four months I had been there. It was nice to talk to my boring boss about something other than how she was still on the fence about the model and color of Saturn she planned to purchase or lease. "Heather, should I go for the four door or the sportier hatchback?" Actually, I see you in something with a larger dashboard so that you can place all your Beanie Babies on it.

As much as I enjoyed appearing in my short business suits, I hated wearing suntan nylons every day. One day I chose to wear a pantsuit so that I didn't have to wear the terribly uncomfortable nylons. In the middle of a meeting, my boss's boss, an older version of my boss, stopped midsentence and said, "Heather, why aren't you wearing nylons?" I quickly came up with an excuse. "I was wearing them, but they tore on a chain-link fence I was climbing over in order to save a cat who was stuck up in a tree. So I quickly switched to slacks so as not to be late," I said, thinking that saving a feline would score me some points. "I just looked down and saw your veiny foot sticking out and it just shook me to my core." She seemed to visibly shiver as she said this. What was the deal with wearing nylons? I hope and pray they never come back in style unless, of course, I develop varicose veins; then I guess I'd welcome them to camouflage my blue bulges. But still they were just so damn constricting, pinching my fat roll right at my waist, and downright itchy. Sometimes during the day I'd start scratching like a dog with fleas.

At the end of a workday, the minute I got into my car in the underground parking lot, I pulled my skirt up, rolled the tight, restricting control-top panty hose down, and then threw them in the back seat of my car and let my flower breathe. I didn't even care that a coworker in accounting got into the car parked next to me as I wrestled with myself to pull them off.

While working at Robinsons May, I lived for the weekend. When five p.m. on Sunday rolled around, I routinely found myself entering a deep depression, which meant either I needed to get a prescription for Valium or face the fact that this was not what I should do with my life. Still, it never occurred to me to quit. I'd never quit anything in my entire life except as a little kid when an unexpected storm blew away my lemonade stand. So I made the best of the two nights and two days before my Mondays came around again.

Saturdays in the fall were great, because just about every other weekend, there was a USC football game to attend. The morning of game day was very busy for me. I had to figure out an outfit that was flattering but not trying too hard, since it was a sporting event. Still, I needed to get a lot of attention once there. I needed comfortable shoes, since there was a lot of walking, but they certainly couldn't be Rockport tennis shoes. It was usually warm in the afternoon but cooled down at night, so I needed something where I could wrap a sweater around my flat ass but not appear like my goal was to camouflage it. Also, I was going back to my alma mater, so every other Saturday was an opportunity to run into someone old or meet someone new, which I did at one particular game.

My girlfriends and I didn't have a lot of money. We relied on guys we'd meet at tailgate parties to provide us with free tickets. We found parking at the residence of either a Crips or Blood gang member's home because that is who lived around the coliseum. They graciously allowed you to park on their lawn for only twenty dollars. No, this wasn't the safest choice for four white sorority girls, but it was a helluva lot cheaper than the USC parking lots, whose extravagant cost would prevent us from having the cash to buy drinks if no guy offered to purchase us a cold beverage. Besides, when we walked around the Crips' hood, we felt secure, as our sorority had sponsored numerous self-protection courses. We all learned how to knee someone in the balls, discovered the power of an elbow to an eyeball socket, and how to yell "*No, No,* and *No*" during confrontations. Also, we had come to the conclusion that gang members who raped USC sorority girls and took their lavaliere (a necklace with your Greek letters on it) as proof to get into the gang was just a rumor started by a whitey to promote bad public relations for the neighboring gang members.

Once we reached the actual coliseum, we bounced around from pre-party to tailgate party, collecting our tickets and free drinks. As my Amstel Light beer buzz set in, so did the heat from the September sun. I felt unstoppable as we walked through the crowded stadium to our seats while being leered and hollered at. Most people were there to see a football game. I was there solely to party and walk the grass runway to show off my new outfit. A USC football game was by far the best singles bar around.

At halftime, the place to go and get drinks was the stand outside of tunnel 26. That is where recent graduates hung out and that's where I met Phil.

Phil and his friend Nick started talking to us as we waited in line for a pretzel. Phil was the best-looking person I'd ever flirted with and he had the "Zed card" to prove it. A Zed card was what models had that showed them in a bunch of different looks on one card for modeling auditions. Phil's Zed card had photos of him as a young dad, as a surfer, and as a doctor holding medical records with a perplexed look on his face. But Phil wasn't just a model for the Ford Modeling Agency; he also specialized in hand modeling. Plus he had a sales position selling industrial parts. He was thirty and had graduated six years before me, and he was even in a great frat. He continued to buy me beers and we never went back to our seats. This was fine with me. I usually held up my two fingers to make the victory sign and participated in the Trojan marching band song. Then I'd get antsy and walk around in a circle where the bathrooms and food stands were until someone else noticed me.

Thank God, I wasn't driving that day, because by the end of the fourth quarter, Phil and I were making out against a graffiti-stained wall outside the coliseum until my friend Tara screamed, "Heather Ann McDonald, what are you doing? We've been looking for you. We're leaving."

"Don't you want to go to Julie's Bar and Grill with Phil and his friend, Nick?" I slurred.

"No. Nick is disgusting and you are coming with us!" Tara wasn't one for mincing words and she physically pulled me away. I managed to hand my Robinsons May assistant buyer business card to Phil. Stumbling all the way back to the hood, passing a couple of makeshift memorials of Jesus candles and empty bottles of Colt 45, was excruciating after drinking since eleven that morning. Now it was dark, but luckily we found our car and made it home safely. I laid down at 7:45 p.m. and didn't budge until the next morning. Once, I got so excited for a party I was throwing that I started drinking way too early and passed out at ten p.m. before many of the guests had arrived. When I woke up the next morning, it was as if I had missed Christmas. I had planned this party for months, and all the old friends who came to see me got to see my butt as I slept in a grain alcohol–induced coma on my bed.

On Monday, Phil called me at work and we talked for a while. I didn't even care that my bitter boss was eavesdropping. I figured if I had to hear her haggle with every Saturn dealership from Santa Ana to Albany, New York, about the cost difference of a car with a sunroof verses one without, then she could listen to me flirt. She had scolded me another time when I went out on a two-hour lunch date with a lawyer who worked downtown. We went to McCormick's and Schmidt's and I knew the lunch was running long, but I wasn't about to give up a three-course meal of shrimp cocktail, Caesar salad, and chicken piccata just because I'd have to face her sour puss.

I realized the only way not to get shit was to make every time I left the office a medical emergency. I started carrying cotton balls and bandages in my purse so that when I returned from an hour and a half lunch where I enjoyed a steak with a stockbroker, I would come back with my arm stretched out with a cotton ball being held by a Band-Aid on the inside of the elbow and a drawn look upon my face. I'd say, "Sorry I had to go to the lab again!" Then when another luncheon date popped up, suddenly I had to take more tests. Coworkers rarely give you grief when leukemia is involved. I was strictly going on those dates for protein, but with Phil I was really interested. Phil asked me out for that Friday and of course I said yes.

On our first couple of dates, we went out to dinner and he paid. I could tell he was a little cheap, so I never ordered a first course, just a main course. I didn't want to rock the boat because I enjoyed being with him. Phil was tall and athletic with a perfectly tan torso, white teeth, dark hair, and he was really fun to talk to. For the third date, he asked if I wanted to come over to his apartment and hang out after work. When I asked what time, he said, "Well, how about eight-thirty?" Making it that late made it clear to me that none of the four main food groups would be offered. I was a little bummed that a meal wasn't included, because I love to eat and have someone else pay for it, but I would do anything to just kiss Phil on his couch and snuggle into his lean neck that smelled of wild coconut. Phil had a nice rent-controlled apartment in Santa Monica and kept it extremely clean. He was anal retentive, to say the least. When he wasn't straightening his tools in his tool chest, he was applying heavy lotions to his moneymaker hands and trimming his cuticles for a potential shoot.

I liked his place and the fact that he had no pets. I hated pretending to love a guy's dog, especially when its wet nose was practically in my clitoris. I didn't know if I should feel flattered or violated. The only thing I experienced that was worse than leaving a guy's house in a little black dress covered in white dog hair was when I dated a guy who owned an overly vocal bird. It didn't matter that he lived in a Malibu beach house. How could I enjoy the waves crashing and relax when every five seconds the bird was squawking, "Will you kiss me? Fuck you! Fuck you! Fuck you cunt"? My nerves were shot after the first thirty minutes. I thought about taking the bird down the street and letting it fly away and then rigging the cage to look like the bird opened it himself, but I was afraid this bird would return to testify against me and say, "Skinny legs try to kill me. . . . Skinny legs try to kill me." I thought about it and realized the innocent bird had to hear the vulgarity somewhere. He didn't just come up with it on his own. Who knows what came out of this guy's mouth when he got angry or when his date didn't put out, which I wouldn't be doing, so in the end Tweety's insults were a warning to get the hell out. Which I did.

Phil asked if I wanted to spend the night and I immediately said, "Yes, but just so you know, I'm not going to have sex with you."

He sweetly said, "That's fine."

Sleeping over at a guy's house was nothing new to me. Some would say it is the ultimate act of blue balling, but I always told the guy up front that I was not going to have sex with him. I learned my lesson my freshman year of college when I went out to Gladstone's in Santa Monica with a guy who lived off campus. He was so drunk I agreed to sleep in his bed, since he couldn't drive me home. He was such an asshole about me not having sex with him, bringing up the fact that he had spent $46 on my piña colada and clam chowder in a sourdough bowl, that I decided to call USC security at three a.m. to come and pick me up and drive me back to my dorm. I told them I was a nurse in training and had to make five a.m. rounds that morning in the trauma unit. Since then, I always made it clear, not that I had never had sex before, but that I wasn't going to have sex on that night. Sleeping at Phil's was fine except that I was so afraid I would snore or drool. I barely closed my eyes all night.

Slowly the dates between Phil and me started to get progressively worse. They no longer included a meal or even a healthy snack such as a Balance Bar. We weren't even seeing each other on the weekends anymore. I had become Miss Monday. We did, however, make plans for him to come to my apartment on a Sunday at five p.m. I was going to make us salmon in dill sauce, rice, and salad for dinner. All of my roommates were out of town. He was going to come by after he was done surfing. Knowing how neat he was and how disgusting our apartment was—with no money for a cleaning service or picking up a Consuelo outside of Home Depot to come and clean—I must have spent six hours scouring every crevice of our place, from the eye shadow embedded in the bathroom tile grout to the never-before-dusted balcony. That didn't even include the amount of time I spent shopping and cooking. Just as I was finishing putting tea roses in a vase—as if we lived like that—the phone rang and it was Phil saying he was still surfing. I acted really casual like I was the cool girlfriend and said, "That's fine. Have fun! I'll see you in an hour or so." I continued polishing, dusting, and rearranging the throw pillows on the twin bed in the living room we used as a couch when the phone rang again and Phil said he was now stuck in a lot of traffic on the Pacific Coast Highway. Again I assured him it was fine and I'd see him when he got there.

Then he called about twenty minutes later and said, "You know, I'm really tired. Can we do this another time?"

"What? Are you kidding me? No! This is so rude of you. I've been waiting here all day for you," I said extremely annoyed.

"OK. I'm coming," he said like the guilty flake he was.

No sooner could I regain my happiness than the phone rang again and it was Phil. "You know what, I'm not coming tonight. I don't think this is working out."

I tried to backpedal and soon ended up begging for him to allow me to come over to his place and talk. I knew I had to tell him that I was a virgin. I knew he was confused, thinking how could this girl who was willing to grind me up against a dirty wall in the middle of the afternoon only hours after meeting still not be having sex with me after numerous dates and sleepovers? At the time, I figured if I could just be honest with him, he'd understand and we could continue to date until we became exclusive and then we'd have sex.

When I got to Phil's place, we sat on the couch together and

I finally said it. "Phil, the reason I have not had sex with you is because I've never had it with anyone. I'm a virgin."

He was very surprised and said, "Wow, I was wondering, Why doesn't this girl have any interest in my penis?" Of course, I'm sure no girl has ever turned down having sex with his penis as many times as I did, especially with those hands of his, which were practically insurable. So I thought by telling him, he would get that I was not rejecting him. I went on to say, "I just want to assure you I'm not saving it for marriage. I just want to be in a boyfriend-girlfriend relationship." I even dropped the "love" part so as to not freak him out, but it was too late. He was freaked.

He looked me straight in the eye and said, "Look, Heather, I think you're a great girl, but I don't want this responsibility."

What responsibility? I'm not asking you to marry me or raise a child with me. But it was out there now, that in order for him to have sex with me like normal people do in their twenties and thirties, he'd have to promise to be my boyfriend. I'm sure he feared that once we did have sex, I'd be impossible to break up with. I left that night devastated and cursing my virginity. Why didn't I just get it over with and sleep with Kevin or any of the other dozen guys in college who skateboarded past me. But then I'd go back in my mind and say no, I want it to be special with someone who really cared about me, and obviously Phil didn't. He didn't even want to come over and have dinner with me at my place on a Sunday night when I had prepared wild salmon from the Copper River.

The following weekend after the breakup, I had no plans,

which depressed me. As I was lying by the pool on Saturday reading *People* magazine, this guy in our building, Clay, started talking to me. We had seen each other a few times, and he and his friend offered me a margarita. Clay and his roommate, Todd, had made a pitcher and brought it down to the pool. Clay was not my type. He was kind of short, had long hair, and was not a college graduate. But as the cheap tequila set in, my mood improved. Then Clay and Todd invited me to a party that they were going to that night in Chatsworth, about a half hour away from the apartment.

"Totally," I said. "Let me just go up and change." As I was putting on my black shorts and fitted black vest, my roommates questioned my sanity.

"Those guys are gross," Tara said.

"Who cares? I have nothing else to do tonight and I want to have fun. Maybe there'll be someone good at the party." I did not want to go back to the cubicle on Monday having done nothing fun all weekend.

The party seemed pretty average to the naked eye. It was a ranch-style family home in the Valley. Most of the people there were older—mid- to late thirties, some forties—and within minutes I knew there were no potential dudes for me. My buzz wore off and I wondered how I was going to hang there all night because Todd had driven the three of us. That's when Clay told me he had brought something for us. He opened a little brown bag and it was mushrooms. I had never tried cocaine, though I'd been offered it many times. I never tried it because I knew it had a reputation for giving you the energy to talk all night and make you not want to eat. Anything that could curb my appetite and inspire me to talk more, most likely about myself, was just too tempting. With that combination, if I even tried it once, I knew I'd become addicted. I tried pot once, but everybody kept yelling at me that I was smoking the bong wrong. I decided it was too technical and no drug is worth having to be criticized. So when I was offered a drug that just required eating it, I felt confident I could do it successfully. Besides, I loved all kinds of mushrooms: white mushrooms, portobello, oysters, shiitake. Why not psychedelic mushrooms, too?

The next thing I knew, I was swimming in the pool and it was not a pool party. I was diving off the diving board fully clothed doing back flips and cannon balls. The only other person who joined me was Clay. I loved swimming in that pool. I did it for hours. I had been on the swim team in elementary school, so I knew all the strokes. I did the breast stroke, the butterfly, and in between was kissing Clay by the waterfall. I was so high that I never noticed that everyone at the party but us was in the porn industry, but I, the virgin, was the crazy one. It made sense: Chatsworth is the porn capital of the world. Even if I hadn't taken the mushrooms, it's not like I knew who these porn stars or directors were. The only porn I'd seen at that point was one starring my sister's childhood friend. We were so curious we had to pop it in the VCR. She was having a three-way with two other girls. Thinking back, probably in that house's living room with the same rock fireplace. I felt bad for our old childhood friend, rubbing and licking and working so hard to get these two other girls off and it was never her turn. I hope she got paid a little extra for that, but fortunately I don't know how the porn union works.

Todd drove us home, and I'm sure he was drunk, but we made it back to Brentwood alive and soaking wet. I don't know what I had said to Clay all night, but he definitely thought he was going to get lucky. I told him to change into dry clothes and I'd do the same, and meet me back at my apartment. The minute I got in my apartment, I locked the door behind me. For at least an hour, Clay called my phone and then ran up and pounded on my door for five minutes. Then he'd go back down and start calling all while I pretended to pass out. The next eight months, I avoided running into him as best I could. I also avoided ordering anything with mushrooms for fear of ending up fully clothed in the deep end of a pool somewhere.

The following Friday, I got a call from the human resources girl at Robinsons May. She said, "Hey, Heather, can you come by and talk? I'm busy now, but how about five p.m.?" "Sure," I said. I didn't think much of it until I saw her coming down the escalator and smiled at her, but when she saw me, she averted her eyes and immediately pretended like she didn't see me. It was just like Penny Baker did when she knew I hadn't made varsity cheerleading. At five o'clock, I went to her office and she said, "Heather, today is the kind of day I hate, because it's going to be your last." She went on to say that Robinsons May and I just weren't a good fit. I think the fact that I hadn't mastered the computer program after ten months on the job didn't help. I burst into tears. What was I going to tell my parents? They had such dreams of me becoming a manager of the Woodland Hills

Robinsons May one day. Within twenty minutes, I was in my car pulling off my smelly, disgusting nylons for the last time, and I felt this overwhelming sense of relief. This was the last time I would ever have to drive on this parking lot. Free at last! Free at last! Lord have mercy—Heather McDonald is free at last!

Now what the hell was I going to do?

I finally decided to do what I always feared: be a waitress while I pursued acting. I had reason to fear it. I can say with confidence that I was the world's worst waitress. To get the job waiting tables I had lied, saying that I had waitressed throughout college. At the restaurant where I worked we'd put the orders in the computers and "runners" would bring the food out for us. Once we were short a runner and I was asked to bring three plates out, which I had no idea how to do, let alone the strength in my weak wrists to balance three large entrées. I quickly thought up another lie and said, "Well, at my last restaurant we had a very strict insurance policy and it was illegal to carry more than two plates at a time." But nothing was more horrifying then the day I took a lunch order at a table that also included lamb chops to go. When I placed the check down the woman looked at me and nicely asked, "Oh, and can you bring our lamb chops to go now, please?" My face turned white. I never had entered the lamb chop order into the computer! I had completely forgotten. The lamb chops took a good twenty minutes to prepare. There was no way to fix this. I went back to the kitchen and started to hyperventilate, while clutching my vagina in fear. I looked back at table 19 sucking on their after-dinner mints and tallying up their bill. These people were actually leaving me a tip. They had no idea. I didn't deserve to live. What if the chops were for their boss? I had ruined two innocent people's livelihoods. If it wasn't for my manager, who talked me down and gave them a complimentary veal marsala to take back with them, I might have ended my life right there.

I had already taken a little stand-up course, so I had a ten-minute act that I could perform at open mikes and small rooms, which I did. That's where I met Dan.

Dan was a thirty-four-year-old divorced dad with a five-year-old son. He was a successful commercial real estate broker whose real passion was stand-up comedy. He had a deal with a restaurant with a back room where they had comedy night once a week. He'd book the comics, which also ensured him a spot to perform. Dan was not my type, especially after supermodel Phil. He was tall and thin, had curly brown hair, and wore glasses. But I thought that maybe I shouldn't go for looks again and instead go for someone who gets me. In turn, Dan thought I was funny, and at this early stage in my comedy career, this was extremely important to me.

I was driving Dan back to his house after we had both performed at a coffee shop when he happened to spot those disgusting suntan nylons in my car. He assumed they came off when I was in the heat of passion with someone. I pulled them out of his hands for fear of any lingering sweaty feet smell and explained about my horrible cubicle job and my recent uninvited departure. He started looking around and asked, "What else do you keep in this car?" Then the real horror set in and Dan said, "Heather, why do you have a boneless uncooked chicken breast in your car? It's going to go bad. What kind of Saran Wrap is this wrapped in? Wait, what is this?"

I turned to see Dan—my new crush—holding one of my silicone breast enhancers in his hand. I had peeled off my breasts after a long sweaty night of dancing at a nightclub the previous week and I had totally forgotten about them. In fact, I had been gossiping with my roommates about how I thought Tara had stolen them when all the while they were under my passenger seat. I tried to grab it, but when he realized what it was, he started to hold it up high and tease me. "Heather, I have your boob. Don't you think it's a little early for us to be going to second base?" I was driving and he was holding it up high, and somehow it fell out of my sunroof and landed on the front window of my Celica. We were now going pretty fast on Santa Monica Boulevard, and the combination of the speed and the adhesive on the tittie cutlet made it clear that this boob was not leaving. I tried to turn on my windshield wipers, but they weren't strong enough to move it. I explained to Dan, "I wasn't pretending I had bigger boobs. I wasn't wearing a bra and didn't want nipple hard-on." As I turned the spray mist on it, the windshield wiper was finally able to push the boob cutlet off all the way into the vehicle driving beside us. The older woman whose lap it landed on looked horrified at the wayward jellyfish as I quickly made a right turn and kissed my one breast goodbye forever.

As embarrassing as that whole scenario was, it also made me realize that I really liked Dan. Even though I had only been doing stand-up for a few months, maybe a fellow comedian was what I really needed. The bonus was that he went to USC, too, just like Phil. I liked dating guys who went to USC. It kept me in that postcollegiate realm and somehow felt like home to me. I liked that Dan had a day job that provided him with a good income. He owned a cute house and took me on very nice dates. One included a helicopter ride over LA straight out of a reality dating show. Instead of two other female contestants, we were with another couple who were his clients. I loved it and I felt so sophisticated. There I was talking in the headphones: "This is amazing! This is so surreal! Look, is that traffic? Wow. Oh my, is that a landfill? Oh never mind, that's just Santa Monica Beach."

When he invited me to a party of an associate, I was thrilled. I loved going to cocktail parties where I knew no one but my date. It was my opportunity to wow the guy by showing how I could talk to anyone. In these situations, I liked to pretend I was a senator's wife. I love role-playing, even if I am the only one in on it. I was just the stunning woman behind the powerful man, cordial and pleasant to everyone but never outspoken. When we arrived at the beautiful colonial home, I felt so regal in my navy Nicole Miller halter dress and gold Chanel knockoff hoop earrings. As we easily found parking, I was a bit surprised that there was no valet, but hopefully it meant these people were down to earth. We approached the dimly lit porch and I began to think, What kind of dull dinner is this? Dan rang the bell and a harried mother holding a tired toddler opened the door.

"Dan, what are you doing here?" she smiled.

"Oh my God, Sheri, was the party . . ."

She cut Dan off. "Ah, the party was last night! We wondered where you were."

"Hi. I'm Sheri?" She said politely as she wiped her toddler's snot off his nose and rubbed her hand clean on her mom jeans.

Wait a minute. This guy, my smart divorced dad, Dan, got the day wrong of a major event that I bought a dress for and put on a credit card that had 17 percent interest and a balance of $8,563.64? Now I was pissed, and even my best impression of a senator's wife could not hide my disappointment. Sheri's husband stepped into the doorway and said, "Hey, Dan, come on in. You're only about twenty-five hours late." Dan started to shake his head, laughing, while he began to head in.

"No." I pulled on Dan's hand. "I'm sure you're exhausted from last night. We're so sorry we missed it." I was appalled that Dan actually wanted to hang out and have drinks and leftover appetizers while we were dressed to the nines and they were in the middle of putting two small children to bed. When we got in the car, I tried to save the evening and my expensive dress, which would cost me more each day it sat on my credit card balance. "Since we're all dressed up, let's go out to dinner, someplace really nice," I suggested, knowing now that a senator's wife usually had many plans on a given night and had to choose between black-tie charity events.

"No, let's just get takeout and go back to my place," he said. I was pretty disappointed but tried to tell myself that Dan just didn't want to share me with an entire restaurant.

As we started to drive back to his place, I knew we would get in the same "I'm not sleeping with you tonight" conversation, and I began to ponder if I should just be honest with him. I brought up the party again.

"Isn't it going to be bad for your business that you had the wrong date and missed that party?"

"Who cares?" Dan said casually. "I'm pretty sure I'm going to move back to San Diego, anyway."

"You are?" I asked. This was the first I had heard about it. What about us? And more important, what about the stand-up room he ran on Thursdays? Dan went on to say that he had already been offered a job and found someone to lease his house. As I followed him back to his house, I thought to myself: This guy has not considered me once in his future plans. I'm just some fun young girl to hang out with. I didn't know what I was going to say or do because I still really liked him and started to feel sad that he was moving.

I began to reason: San Diego is only two hours away. Maybe it could work. I could go down on the weekends that he didn't have his son and then eventually maybe he would introduce me to him and possibly say, "Now Heather is not going to try to replace your mom. She could never do that because she is two whole dress sizes smaller." I was being very quiet as we entered his house.

"Can I hang up my coat?" I asked.

"Of course. There's a closet right there," he said as he headed into the kitchen with our take-out dinner. I was still a little dazed by how the night turned out, but nothing could have prepared me for what I found next. As I opened the hall closet door, there it hung, a USC Marching Band uniform. Ew, Dan was in the marching band? As much as I loved rocking out to the marching band at games, it was a certain type of guy who was in the band, and that type of guy was not my type. Dan knew it and that is why he didn't tell me. Well, if he chose not to disclose his affiliation with the marching band, then I was certainly not going to disclose my affiliation with virginity. I decided then and there that we were done. I pulled out the marching band uniform and walked into the kitchen with a sense of purpose and said, "You were in the marching band and didn't tell me? Yet I'm not good enough to meet your five-year-old son—me, the former social chairman and co–vice president of rush. I don't think so, buddy! See ya!"

When I got home, there was a message from Dan explaining that he had played the trumpet in high school and only did it because a partial scholarship was involved. I didn't even want to hear the rest of it. I was glad it was over. He wasn't my type and had a lot a baggage and trumpet paraphernalia. I thought I was doing some charitable work by dating him when he—who was in the band and probably only dated the girls who also wore the polyester band uniform throughout college—still didn't think I was girlfriend-worthy.

I continued to send my head shots out during the day to various casting ads I'd read in *Dramalogue,* a weekly magazine for beginning actors to find out about open calls for shows and plays. The thing about this magazine was anyone could put an ad in it. No one was doing background checks on advertisers, and I didn't have John Walsh's personal digits. It was a little sketchy. Finally, I got a call for an independent nonunion short film. It required that I Rollerblade, which I could, but the producers wanted me to come down to North Hollywood (which is not even near the real Hollywood) and bring my blades to show off my moves. I felt hopeful about the audition. It was my first one since I was fired from Robinsons May, and I got it without an agent! What a go-getter I was. I knew the gig was unpaid, but I would get the tape from it, and any talent agent wanted to see you on film before they would sign you. The catch-22 was that without an agent, it's very hard to book an acting job where you could get that precious tape. I hoped that this gig would give me what I needed.

When I arrived at the "production" office, it was a small non-air-conditioned room in a two-story dilapidated building. Inside were framed posters of movies I had never heard of like *Turtle Nation* and *Mucus Island.* The producers explained that these were their movies and that they go straight to video and do really well overseas. After they watched me Rollerblade up and down Lankershim Boulevard for ten minutes, they broke the amazing news that I had the part. "What exactly is the role I'll be playing?" I asked. I wanted to really prepare and find out what made this Rollerblading character tick, create a backstory, find her motivation . . . gee, did she even have an accent?

The older man said, "Sadie here wrote the film, and it's based on a dream she had. That's all you really need to know." Sadie was a redhead in her late thirties who looked like she'd been ridden pretty hard.

"So you don't have a script I can read?" I asked.

"No. Just meet us here on Saturday at ten a.m.," she said firmly. "We'll all drive together to the location." She added, "Oh, and bring a couple of string bikinis, preferably G-strings that wardrobe can look over." In the end, all I knew was that

I was going to be Rollerblading and wearing a bathing suit. I only brought one-pieces, assuring my stomach would not be featured. I thought it didn't sound so bad and that it might actually be a good clip for my acting reel. Maybe there was a guest spot on *Baywatch Nights* in my future?

I arrived at the offices at my precise call time of ten a.m. only to sit outside for another thirty minutes before the old man arrived. He had long gray hair, a beard, and was probably in his late fifties. He looked like a member of the Grateful Dead. When it was time to go, Sadie, the cameraman, the old man, and I climbed into a compact two-door Honda Accord.

"Where are we going?" I asked as I put my Rollerblades in the hatchback.

The old man, who was driving, said, "We're going to pick up Cassie." Another person was going to fit in this tiny car? Where was my left thigh going to go? We drove for about forty minutes until we stopped at a gas station. The old man announced, "Hey, get anything you want. It's on me." This was his idea of craft services. I was still trying to be the cool hardworking actress who never complained, so I took a little bag of nuts. At the gas station, as I sat in the car nibbling on my cashews, my window was tapped and a cute brunette about my age was standing there. I opened my door and she introduced herself as Cassie. I didn't know if she lived at the gas station or what, but I felt a little relieved that another girl was dumb enough to be doing this gig.

I sat on the hump between Cassie and the cameraman, and my head kept hitting the roof as we drove up into a bumpy wooded area until we finally parked. "OK, this is it," the old man said gleefully. We followed him past NO TRESPASSING signs and then did some serious crouching down through a broken chain-link fence that caught onto my ponytail and pulled me back so that I fell on my ass and dropped my skates.

"How much farther?" I asked nearly out of breath.

"Oh, it's right down here," Jerry Garcia said as he steadied his balance on a tree branch. I looked up and saw an empty reservoir. We had to slide down on our butts to get to the bottom. This was just paying my dues, which was essential to making it in Hollywood, right?

The next thing I knew, I was Rollerblading up and down the reservoir wearing only a high-cut sparkly blue one-piece bathing suit, warming up my skating skills for the big shoot. Then the cameraman told Sadie and the old man that he was ready to shoot. Sadie said, "OK, Heather, you need to put this on." And she handed me a huge frog mask that covered my entire head down to my collarbone. It looked very familiar to me and I realized it was in one of those movie posters in their office named *Frog Freaks*. It did not occur to me to object to putting a thick rubber frog head on in 100-degree weather or to bring up the fact that we could be arrested for trespassing on government property. The same way I didn't say anything the time a male masseur worked out all the knots in my breasts. I did as I was told, put on the mask, and did some turns as the cameraman, who was also on skates, followed me. Besides barely being able to breathe through the green rubber, I could hardly see. My peripheral vision was impaired and I could not see my feet or the bump that was just ahead of me that made me fall straight onto my face. Luckily the warts on the mask protected my forehead. Now I was injured and my knee was bleeding. "The crew" tossed me some paper towels, but all I cared about was whether you could tell it was me. Was I really just another five-foot-ten-inch-tall 34C-size frog on Rollerblades in the Sylmar reservoir?

On our ride back, Sadie handed Cassie and me a script. The old man said, "I've got some doctors who want to invest in this one, so I have to start shooting next week. Maybe you girls would like to read for it."

"Does it involve either frogs or Rollerblading?" I asked.

"No, this is the real deal, a feature." I started reading over Cassie's shoulder. One page in, I read a stage direction that said, "Carla applies suntan lotion on Stephanie's back. Stephanie turns over and Carla applies suntan lotion on her naked breasts."

"Wait, so do Stephanie and Carla have bathing suits on?" I questioned.

"No, but it's very tasteful," replied Sadie.

"Well, I'm not doing anything where I'm nude or which involves nudity. It has always been in my clause when I've done legitimate work that involved having a clause of some sort," I stated matter-of-factly.

"Oh, come on. Everybody does nude scenes. What? You don't think Michelle Pfeiffer was sucking cock on film before she was in *Grease 2*? You think you're going to win an Oscar, Heather?" Sadie argued.

"I don't know, but I don't want to win a PAC [Porn Academy Award]." There was an uncomfortable silence. I didn't want to be totally unhelpful, so I piped up: "In case you guys are looking for a location, I know a great house in Chatsworth with a fabulous pool and a really springy diving board. I can get it for you for a discount!"

Once home, I literally licked my wounds. I decided that until I had an agent or a manager, I would go back and work for my parents selling houses during the day and do my stand-up at night. I found out about a six-week class on getting more real estate business and improving your overall life. What caught my eye was that at the end of the six weeks everyone went skydiving. I guess the idea was to inspire us to look down at all the real estate we'd be selling. I had always wanted to go skydiving and felt this was the perfect opportunity because my parents agreed to pay for the course under the pretense that I was learning the business and it was, of course, a business write-off.

Daniel Penn ran the class. He was the poor man's Tony Robbins. He was from the South, very tan, fit, blond highlighted tips with a fresh set of capped white teeth to top off his look of success. He began the class with a story about his early days in real estate: "Don't y'all just hate door knocking? Well, my first day in real estate, my office manager told me to go door knocking. So the first house I knocked on, when the owner answered, I said, 'Hi. My name is Daniel Penn, and I want to sell your house,' and he slammed the door in my face. So you know what I did? I ran around to his back door and knocked, and when the man opened that door, I said, 'Hi. I'm Daniel Penn, and some jerk just slammed the door in my face.' Well, he laughed and we had coffee, and I sold that house and three others for him, because you know why? One, conceive it, see it. Two, believe it, say it. Three, achieve it, be it! People, that's right. Because I wasn't always the most successful real estate agent in the San Fernando Valley making over four hundred thousand dollars a year, no. But today I am, and you can be, too!"

For the next six weeks, Daniel went on to tell us how he woke up every morning at six to meditate, work out, and write down his plan of attack for the day. He lost credibility with me when I called him at nine a.m. to ask him a question. Finally, after four rings, he picked up the phone, and his voice sounded so groggy I couldn't even detect his Southern drawl. He tried to sell the class on private life coaching sessions. I think it takes a lot of audacity to call yourself a life coach. Every life coach I've ever encountered has been divorced at least once and only became a life coach because they failed at their other careers in life. What qualifies them to be a life coach? They like to shop at the Container Store and label shit? I didn't care to associate with Daniel Penn after the class ended. All I cared about was the field trip to Perris, California for skydiving.

Once I arrived in Perris, I was shocked to find out it was going to cost me $185. I was under the distinct impression that it was included as part of the life-changing real estate course. What was I going to do, not put my credit card down? Besides, I wasn't paying cash. It was on a credit card to be paid off in the way, way future, unless I died while skydiving, then essentially the skydiving was free because as a dead person I was never going to pay off the card. I didn't complain, especially because I was a little hungover from the night before. It was tandem jumps, so I would be attached to an extremely experienced sky-diver trained and certified to do these jumps. I would be in front with my skydiver behind me like a human backpack.

As long as it wasn't up to me and it was someone else's re-sponsibility to save my life, I felt relieved. I feel the same about a person bobsledding. I'd be fine so long as I am the person in the back hunched over praying. We watched a little skydiving training video and then they taught us how to pull the string to release the parachute. After the fifteen-minute training session concluded, I had a few hours to kill until my group went into the plane. I laid out on a blanket and fell asleep working on my tan until I was awakened by Carol, one of the other realtors in the group.

"Come on, Heather. Our group is up next. You have to get into your jumpsuit." Within minutes our plane was taking off. I must say, in my jumpsuit I looked a lot like Jaime Sommers, aka the Bionic Woman. It wasn't my typical outfit. Instead of my platform wedge heels, I went for the combat khaki hiking boots they provided. It was a bit of an adrenaline rush just being all hooked up like that. The plane was specifically designed for sky-diving. We all sat on a hard metal bench facing one another like we were real Marine paratroopers ready to invade the Middle East. It wasn't until this point that I was completely sober and realized that this was not a Six Flags Magic Mountain ride. I was jumping out of a fucking airplane. As the plane continued to fly higher, my skydiver, Amy, a cute twenty-five-year-old girl just one year older than me, began to attach herself to the straps around my torso. She was like hugging me from behind. As she did this, she started to talk to Mark, the skydiver attached to my friend Carol. We had been told Mark held the world record for the most tandem jumps ever.

Amy said, "Mark, I'm so pissed. It's three-thirty and it's my first jump of the day. That's bullshit."

Mark replied, "Amy, you just got certified this past Sunday! You are on the bottom of the totem pole because of your lack of experience. Of course, they're going to give the veteran divers more tandem jumps. It's only fair."

When I heard that, my stomach started feeling really nervous, like I needed to take a big shit. What the hell am I doing? I thought. I didn't have a lot to live for when I signed up six weeks ago. Part of my attitude was that life would never get better than it was for me in college. If I died, at least I had fun so far. I don't know if some of Daniel Penn's inspirational talk did seep in, but suddenly I was hopeful for my future. I thought maybe I could make it doing something I loved—stand-up comedy and acting—and I didn't want to die a virgin! How bad would that suck? My mother was so proud of this fact that she'd probably put it on my tombstone. It would read, "Loving daughter, sister, aunt, and virgin. May she rest in peace with her hymen still intact."

No. I don't want to do this. Why couldn't I have Carol's pro Mark with all of his tandem jumping experience? Had I not passed out in the sun, maybe I would have learned that Amy had tandem parked more times than she'd tandem jumped.

At this point, the tandem groups started to stand up and walk toward the open door. I couldn't hear what they were saying when they stood at the edge of the plane. But I could tell they were counting as they rocked back and fourth, "One, two, three," then they'd jump and disappear. Whenever a group left, a single skydiver with a video camera jumped out after them to catch the fall on tape. I thought, Oh great. I'll finally get the tape I need for my acting reel. Ironically it's just me falling to my death. No matter how dramatic it is, it's going to be difficult to book acting jobs when I'm dead. Maybe I'll make the six o'clock evening news and they'll show my head shot, since there are three hundred in my backseat right now. That will be the highlight of my career. It was almost our turn as we took tiny steps together to the edge. I looked out at the clouds below me and Amy started to rock us back and forth as we said, "One, two," and then she suddenly pushed me out into the atmosphere. The bitch didn't even wait to get to three! But to her credit maybe she knew I was considering bracing the sides and chickening out, and then she wouldn't even get one jump in for the day and she really needed it to build up her jumping résumé.

As I spread my arms and legs out like a frog as instructed, I realized that maybe playing a Rollerblading-bathing-suit-wearing frog had helped me somehow for this very moment. The air felt so refreshing against my skin. Of course, in the video, it's that refreshing air that caused my cheeks to flap in the wind. I'm sure it would look great on my reel if I was auditioning for the part of half woman/half blowfish.

After what seemed to be about twenty seconds, Amy told me to pull our parachute's cord. But I couldn't move my arms; the wind pressure was so strong. I told her to do it, and when she did, we were expelled into space like a rocket. The contraption holding the shoot that fit on the outside of my jumper sucked up toward my vagina with such pressure that I had terrible inner thigh bruises for weeks afterward. When noticed, skydiving was not the first explanation that came to people's minds.

As Amy and I floated down, I knew we were safe and I finally relaxed. We talked about the restaurant Amy worked at, how she skydived the first time just thirteen months ago. I pretended to be impressed instead of pissed that my life was in the hands of an amateur tandem jumper. I couldn't blame anyone. I put myself in that position because of my lack of self-esteem by having such little faith in my future.

In the end, it wasn't the smoothest landing, much like the rest of my life at this point, but I was happy knowing I had lived through air trauma. I fell on my knee and bruised it again just like my recent close-up as a relative of Kermit. Nevertheless, I was alive and determined to make a life for myself in which I would never feel the need to skydive again. From now on, I would remain seated in airplanes, preferably first class, or at United economy with extra leg room space, and I would do this by working hard, pursuing my dream, or marrying someone rich, whichever presented itself first.

About eight months later, things were going well. I was making money in real estate and performing stand-up. When I ran into Phil again at the beach, I was feeling pretty confident. In those days, I actually used to swim in the Pacific Ocean. I mean swim—like I could have been eaten by a shark. I went deep. I liked that people were impressed not only by my wet hair, but that I also body surfed. My motivation for getting in the water was usually twofold. First, I liked the way ocean water made my hair wavy and gave it natural highlights; and second, I needed to pee. Immediately after consuming any liquid, I felt you could see it in my stomach as it began to pooch out. Therefore, peeing it out into the vast ocean waters allowed my stomach to return to its flattest state.

As I came out of the water tanned, soaking wet, with a flat stomach like a brunette Bo Derek in the movie *10* minus the cornrows, Phil was standing there with a big smile on his face. I acted as nice and friendly as ever and told Phil and the couple he was with all about my stand-up and what I'd been up to. I invited the three of them to see me at the Belly Room in the Comedy Store the following night. Besides wanting to impress Phil with my witty routine, I needed to bring at least three people with me in order for them to allow me to perform. I hadn't met anyone new that week, so this was perfect.

Phil called the next day to get the details of where my big show was. In the conversation the subject of my virginity just naturally came up.

"So have you dated anyone seriously since we went out?" he asked.

"Yes, I did, but I recently broke up with him," I said with confidence.

Technically I did break up with "Divorced Dad Dan from the Marching Band," as my girlfriends and I would often refer to him. But I knew what he was hinting at, so I just went for it and said, "If you're wondering if I'm still a virgin, you can just keep wondering."

"I don't think you are anymore," he said with intrigue.

"I think you may be right," I said as I gave a sexy giggle afterward.

Yes, that's correct. I was lying. I really don't know why. I guess I wanted him to think he missed out and that I boned the shit out of the very next guy after him. Hopefully, Phil regretted blowing me off.

That night, Phil and the couple came to see me. There were some pretty dreadful comics before me. Following bad acts always makes me nervous that the crowd will begin to tire and start to leave before I get up on stage, but luckily they didn't. As I performed my routine, my three audience members laughed a lot. Afterward, the four of us had drinks and I was on fire, making sassy remarks, whipping out one-liners, making fun of Phil and his hand modeling career much to his friends' delight.

At the end of the night, Phil walked me to my car and we made out up against it. He tasted and smelled as delicious as ever, and I loved feeling that perfect body wrapped around me. He asked me to come over, but as much as I wanted to dry hump all night, I wanted to get a real date out of it, so I said, "No, I'm too tired tonight. What about tomorrow night?" Phil agreed and he called the next day. We made plans for him to come pick me up and take me out to dinner.

At dinner at Crocodile Café, I felt the conversation was going great. I continued to make jokes and jabs at Phil and our relationship. I was having a blast. I felt so confident. I loved the fact that he believed I was no longer a virgin, so he wasn't afraid to pursue me. Who knows—if we continued to date, maybe I would lose it to him without him knowing it. After dinner I assumed we'd go back to his immaculate apartment and see where things would take us. When he passed his own street in Santa Monica and began heading toward Brentwood, I said, "Don't you want to hang out at your place? You know, my roommates are all home."

"I know they are. I'll just drop you off," he said.

"Why? What's wrong? Do you have to rest your hands and make sure they get their full eight hours of beauty rest for their close-up tomorrow?" I joked.

"No, I think you're just a little too much for me right now. I thought it after the comedy club but wondered if you were just coming off your comedy high or something. But after tonight, I think we should just be friends."

I was shocked. He believed I was no longer a virgin, meaning sex was most likely around the corner, but I went so out of my way to prove how confident I was that I became downright obnoxious and a turnoff?

That was the last I saw or heard from Phil. However, I swore I spotted his thumb and forefinger on a coffee mug in a Folgers coffee commercial, and every time I heard, "The best part of waking up is Folgers in your cup," I felt a sting of nostalgia but no regrets.

 Video Vixen

After finishing a truly decent stand-up set at a half Chinese, half Mexican restaurant where you could get taquitos dipped in sweet-and-sour sauce, the emcee, a woman in her late thirties—who did her own routine about her Russian mother performing LL Cool J's rap songs—approached me at the bar. "You vetty, vetty funny," she said in her heavy accent. "Jew know I book other vrooms around dis town."

"Great. I'd love to get up more often."

She continued in her broken Russian. "Me also produce vetty, vetty small vilms. You have a veel with acting scenes you done?"

Again with the freakin' reel, no, no, and no—not unless you want to view me losing in a Miss Tarzana Pageant, choosing an Israeli real estate developer on *Studs,* or Rollerblading in a one-piece bathing suit with a frog head on in the Sylmar reservoir.

She seemed fine with the fact that I didn't have a "veel" and gave me her address to come by and drop off my head shot.

The next day, I found myself parking in front of her gray stucco building with huge "For Rent" red banners hanging around it. I walked past the security gate, which had been propped open by a brick, straight through to the pool area that had been drained except for a small puddle of brown water in the deep end with a few leaves floating on it. I imagined the awkward pool party conversation that must have gone on. "Is your pool salt water or sewer?" I walked up the steps made of tiny pebbles until I found her apartment on the second floor. Before I knocked, I could hear her screaming to someone in her Russian accent.

She opened the door with a phone in one hand and a cigarette in the other. "Heather, honey, ya come in. Come. Come!" She went back to talking on the phone. "That it, $150 a video or . . ." then some more in Russian, then . . . "vuck you." Finally, she hung up, lit a new Eve 100, and turned her attention to me. "Listen, you vetty, vetty funny and you vetty pretty, too. I make dees videos." Then she stressed, "No! Not porno! Nothing like dat, but it's vetty easy money. What size shoe you vear?"

I answered, "A nine." I was a little confused about what was happening, but when someone asks me a question, my initial reaction is to answer truthfully.

"Ah, dat's OK. You can vit into an eight, vight?" she asked, puffing on her cigarette covered in her red lipstick while creating smoke rings the size of bangle bracelets.

"Well, gosh. I'm pretty much a nine," I said. I mean there

was that one year my mom skipped going to the shoe store for new shoes and my feet had grown from a five to a seven. Subsequently, both my big toes are really codependent on the other four toes leaning right up against them. It's not like I was a Geisha girl; it's just that we didn't get around to hitting Buster Browns that year. So I really preferred not to go smaller for fear that my toes would end up literally on top of each other like a pile-up on the 405.

At this point, she had left the room to go down the hall and returned with a pair of black patent leather five-inch-high stilettos. "Here, try?" she said as she held them out for me to take.

I replied, "Actually I can bring my own shoes that fit. By the way, what is this for?"

"One of my clients, a veal sick vuck, like to see girls in high heels crush da bugs. He tired of seeing my veet do it, so I video you doing for ten minutes and you get da fifty bucks. You try them on," she pressed. "They vetty pretty shoes!"

Now, this is where growing up in the Valley with two parents who I have a great relationship with came in handy. I was never going to be that desperate for fifty bucks. If necessary, I could always move back home. It wasn't like I was from Wyoming and would have to board a bus and be humiliated to return home to my small town and explain to customers at the Dairy Queen why I didn't make it as a movie star. When I told the Russian woman I wasn't interested, she tried to convince me to do it by telling me that she kept the bugs in a glass cage. I would stand in an enclosed area where she would dump the bugs and I would stomp on them like Lucille Ball crushing grapes in the classic episode. The Russian explained to me that they were an assortment of cockroaches and crickets and they didn't bite.

I immediately thought of PETA and knew this was a violation of their bylaws or whatever their governing laws were. In general, I was pretty freaked out by bugs and I knew this could not go on my prestigious reel. After having portrayed an amphibian on skates, I felt a bit of kinship with all living creatures. I also heard her say that she made $150 for each video, which meant she was going to pocket $100 when I was the marquis star! Screw that! I thought. Besides, I always had a soft spot for critters ever since I made them in my Creepy Crawlers baking set. I finally thanked the Russian chick for thinking of me and left. As I got in my Celica and began to drive away, I started to feel really bad for the bugs. If the actors weren't even getting a fifty-fifty cut, think of the poor bugs risking their lives to be on camera. I imagined one bug standing on the tip of the pump in front of all the other bugs holding a small sign made out of cardboard and black marker with just the word UNION on it.

After enduring yet another career highlight, I decided to audition for The Groundlings theater, a sketch comedy and improvisation school. I had been accepted to another improvisation school in the Valley and they said I would be able to perform for audiences within months. The Groundlings required you to take four different classes. In each one, the instructor could either pass you, have you retake it, or say, "This isn't the place for you." I was so anxious to "make it" and be seen by the industry as soon as possible. I told my mom I was going to enroll in the

Valley theater, thinking she'd be thrilled to see me on stage that much sooner. Instead, she said, "Heather, The Groundlings is the best. Don't you want to be with the best?" I'm so glad I took her advice, because good improvisation is dependent on all the actors in a group knowing what they're doing.

I loved The Groundlings. It's located on Melrose, and there were always cool bars and restaurants to go to after class. The first time I saw a performance there was on a Sunday night when the B-team performed. Will Ferrell did a sketch where he worked at an amusement park and sang everything that came to mind. Will had gone to USC, too, and had performed legendary pranks that I remembered hearing about. He was in the Delta Tau Delta fraternity. Besides laughing my ass off, I also realized: These people are normal. They're not creepy, overly artistic theater people. They're just funny. Plus, they were human and not insects. I liked the idea of working with humans for a change.

I started level one the following week. It consisted of basic improvisation games. Then level two was more about writing characters and monologues. It took about a year to get to level three, where we performed. We presented the sketches and monologues we wrote and included some improvisation, where we'd get suggestions from the audience and use this to create a scene. Of course, my family and close friends were all there. After the show, I felt fantastic. Everyone loved my character based on my Aunt Clare from the Hamptons having a martini at a wedding. She dissected every aspect of the wedding to another guest with lines like, "And the bride wearing stark white, not even a cream color, she's six months pregnant, who is she fooling? I'm not one to gossip, but is the groom even certain he's the father?" I was eager to attend the after party at my fellow cast member Jen's house and looked forward to lots of compliments.

Jen shared a rental house off Laurel Canyon. As I was parking on the steep hill, I noticed a very good-looking guy getting out of a Porsche, which was a few years old, but a Porsche nonetheless. I had dated a Mercedes, a few BMWs, and a Ferrari, but never a Porsche, so naturally I was intrigued. At the party, we began talking, and Porsche introduced himself as Jason. He said he had been friends with Jen for a few years. He had seen the show and thought I was great. Since I thought I was great, too, we already had a lot in common. He told me how he had finished law school but did not pass the bar the first time and needed to take it again. I reminded him that JFK Jr. had to take it three times before he passed. He said he had to get going, but he hadn't asked for my number. I must have been super confident after nailing that last improvisation about a Laundromat, where I showcased my incredible skills by folding towels in the air as I spoke in a Southern accent, because I said to him, "So are you going to ask for my number or what?"

Jason said, "Ah yeah, sure. What is your number?" I wrote it down for him to ensure there were no mistakes. I added as he walked out the door, "You better call me."

Jen later approached me and let me know that they were just friends, but at one time they did date. I told her I was fine with it as long as she was, and even though she said she was, she seemed a bit hesitant. Jen and I liked each other, but we weren't that close. No one at Groundlings even knew I was a virgin. I just acted like, of course, I've had sex with boyfriends. I joked that I would never sleep with a guy whose bed was a futon, because in order to get with me, you needed to have a proper mahogany carved headboard.

Jason called the next day from the law office where he worked and we made plans for him to pick me up at my apartment. I shared it with my sister Shannon, who was also a lawyer but had passed the bar on the first try. (She was a little smarter than JFK Jr.) Once she finished law school in Northern California, she moved back to LA and we decided to live together. When it came to splitting up the phone bill, it was a lot nicer doing it with someone who was calling the same parents as I was. At dinner, Jason told me that he owned a house in Santa Monica that his parents bought for him when he started law school. I loved that he lived in Santa Monica and owned property, but I was disturbed to find out that while he was a proud homeowner, his parents were forced to rent. He was an only child and apparently very spoiled. What parents in their fifties would buy a property for their son when they couldn't afford to buy one for themselves? It reminded me of another only child I knew in high school who got a brand new VW Rabbit convertible for her sixteenth birthday while both her parents drove clunkers. I asked Jason if he felt any guilt accepting such a nice home, but he insisted that his parents loved living in their one-bedroom rental.

Jason and I went on quite a few dates and he always treated me to a gourmet dinner, and he always wore a suit, which I loved, because it meant I could get more dressed up, too. The one thing that bothered me about his looks were his crooked teeth. I wish his parents would have paid for an orthodontist to straighten out his smile instead of giving him a house. One night after dinner, he asked if I wanted to meet his parents at a jazz club for a drink. They were very nice and seemed very much in love for being married all those years.

Jason later told me that his mom took off with another man when he was five and didn't return for two years. Ever since, his parents remained together. I hate knowing people's sexual history, because when I talked to them, it was all I could think about. This was true whether it was our neighbor who cheated on her husband with her preacher or a fellow female stand-up who was married to a man, but I knew that she used to go down on a female comic when she opened for her on the road. It's just so distracting to me. I know that women can be switch hitters. I don't believe men can, because with men, as they say, "Once you go dick, you never go back for a lick." It made me sad for Jason imagining him at five and his mom suddenly moved out. Maybe that's why he was so spoiled. She must have felt tremendous guilt for leaving him.

Jason and I had been dating about a month and a half when the holidays approached. I was excited to have a date for New Year's Eve and actually have someone to kiss instead of avoiding some gross guy by huddling with my girlfriends in a corner. The only other time I had been asked out on New Year's Eve was by a thirty-four-year-old escrow officer I met at my parents' office Christmas party when I was nineteen. I was so excited to get all dressed up and go to a fancy restaurant, maybe go dancing after, until he called that night around six p.m. and said he was going to pick me up and bring me back to his house in Palmdale, where he was going to make pasta for us. The only thing that sounded worse than the date rape I was sure would happen was the crappy spaghetti I was going to have to pretend to like. Besides, no one would be able to hear my screams, Palmdale is way out in the boonies. I called him back a half hour later, said I had broken out in a full-body rash, and never spoke to him again.

I told Jason about a charity event we went to every year. It included drinks and a buffet and was $110 a person. He seemed enthusiastic to go. Then he asked what I was doing for Christmas. I told him how we always had Christmas Eve and Christmas dinner at my parents' house with the immediate family. He hinted that he was available on Christmas Eve, so after checking with my parents, I invited him.

I started to think Jason could be the one for me. He was successful. He wasn't in the business—which was good because his work as an attorney was steadier—but he was supportive of what I did. He told me how much he was looking forward to giving me my present on Christmas Eve. I tried not to get carried away about my gift. After conferring with numerous girlfriends, I decided to spend $100 on a black leather wallet for him. Nothing too personal, but who couldn't use a new wallet?

Finally, on Christmas Eve, in front of my entire family, I opened my gift. It was a cappuccino maker, "because you love cappuccinos," he said gleefully. I wasn't expecting a ring, but how about earrings or a charm necklace. I would have appreciated something with deeper meaning than espresso beans.

After dinner, where everyone behaved and got along famously, I walked him out to his car. I got in the car with him and we made out passionately. That's when he asked me, "Heather, when was the last time you were with someone?" I felt comfortable, buzzed, in love, and as joyful as an elf on Christmas Eve. I said, "I haven't been. You would be my first." If this was a reality show, the editor would have put in the ever-present *screech* sound of a needle scratching a record.

Jason was in utter shock. "Oh, really? Why didn't you tell me sooner?" he questioned.

"Because you never asked," I said as I leaned in and tried to continue to make out with him. He kind of pushed my hands away. "I hope that is OK. I just haven't met someone I care that much about before," I said.

"No, it's fine. It's just getting late and your parents are probably wondering what you're still doing out here, so Merry Christmas," he said, looking like he couldn't pull out of the driveway soon enough.

"OK, I'll talk to you tomorrow after I make my first cappuccino," I said with a wink.

That night, I went to bed completely in love and relieved that I told Jason the truth. I was certain he was falling in love with me as well, and soon we'd have sex and in a few years get married. The next day, Christmas, we spoke, but only briefly. He was in between family parties. The day after that, I left a message but didn't hear back from him. I didn't think much of it and called again and got him.

"Jason, so for New Year's Eve, how do you want to pay?" I

felt weird asking him that, but I figured he'd want to buy both of our tickets.

He said, "I don't know. It's a lot of money for New Year's Eve."

I felt a little panicked. I wanted to have a boyfriend for the special night, so I said, "Well, I can put it on my card for both of us. You've gotten so many dinners. Let me get this?"

"Look, I need to study for the bar. It's in three weeks," he argued.

"Are you really going to study on New Year's Eve?" I countered like Angie Harmon in an episode of *Law & Order.*

"Yes, I need to. You just go with your friends. I'm going to have dinner with my parents and then just study as long as I can stay up."

"OK," I said. I was so disappointed but tried to look on the bright side. He was committed to passing the bar this time, and it was great that he was close to his parents. I mean, it wasn't like he was going to some other raging New Year's Eve party with a bunch of guys to pick up chicks.

When New Year's Eve finally arrived, I anxiously put on my dark green velvet minidress from BCBG that I specifically bought with Jason in mind and went to the party. Halfway through the night, I ran into a sorority sister of mine, Patty. Patty was two years older than me and had once made a very racist comment to me at the USC pool. She said, "Heather, how can you stand living in the Valley?" I took a deep breath and began to explain that it only gets really hot for a couple of months a year but that we had a big pool and central air. She cut me off and said, "No, I mean because there are so many Jews there. That's why we moved to Phoenix." I was appalled. I had never heard anything like that before in my life about the Valley. Of course, there were Jews there, along with blacks, Mexicans, Asians, Persians, gays, and everything else America has to offer. We were a potpourri of domestic suburban bliss.

Jason knew Patty through mutual friends, and when her name came up, I relayed that story and thought nothing of it. At the New Year's Eve party, Patty came up to me and said, "Heather, I can't believe you called me a racist. My friends told me what you said when you were at their house with Jason."

I said, "Well, I did not call you a racist, but I did relay a conversation we had where you made a comment about Jews." Of course, I was dying. There is nothing worse than being caught having talked about someone by the same someone who you had talked about. I tried to make it better by saying, "It's not like I said you denied the Holocaust ever happened. I just said your family did not enjoy Jewish neighborhoods."

She tried to deny it and told me how her family had a dear friend who was a Jewish jeweler who always got them gems at wholesale. I finally just apologized for speaking about her without her being there to defend herself. When we were all made up and powdering our faces in the ladies room, Patty turned to me and said, "And I'm sorry to hear about you and Jason."

"What?" I asked.

"Yes, we saw him a couple of nights ago and he said you guys had broken up. Too bad."

My stomach dropped. I couldn't believe it. We're through.

That's it, and he's been telling everyone but me? I tried to cover and said, "Yes, he's just so busy having to retake the bar and all. You do know he failed the first time." Fortunately, Patty the racist did not know he had failed before, so I got a little satisfaction ripping the lid off that one. After she left the bathroom, I went into a stall. I tried to talk myself into enjoying the rest of the night and finding someone cute to make out with, but I couldn't. I just wanted to go home. I told my friends what had happened and took a cab by myself. When I got home, I cried so hard that I threw up. I was sober, so throwing up without my typical alcohol level was new to me.

The next day, I called Jason and told him what Patty had said.

He said in an exhausted tone, "Heather, I just have to focus on passing the bar. I can't have a girlfriend right now."

"OK, well I will never call you again then." I said matter-of-factly.

To which he said, "I would appreciate that."

I hung up. I would appreciate that! My pleasure, mother-fucker. He truly had broken my heart. Luckily I had never opened the cappuccino maker and promptly returned it that day. It cost $106, but since I was returning it with no receipt, I only got $79.99—the after-Christmas markdown. At least I got eighty bucks out of the deal. I knew he dumped me because of my virginity. He just didn't want to deal with it, I guess. Later I talked to Jen, my friend from The Groundlings who introduced us. I told her how he so abruptly dumped me after Christmas, saying he couldn't have a girlfriend after he basically invited himself to my house on Christmas Eve. I offered up the fact that we had not had sex but did not tell Jen I was a virgin.

She said, "Oh, Heather, thank God you didn't have sex with him. He has the smallest penis I've ever seen. I made the mistake of having sex with him, and honestly, I asked, 'Is it in?' and to my horror it was. I wanted to warn you, but I didn't think you guys would have hit it off like you did."

I told Jen about the one night I ended up attempting to give Jason a hand job, but I gave up halfway through because I thought it was never getting hard because it was so small. It was barely the length of my thumb.

The realization that Jason suffered from having an extremely small penis did make me feel better about being dumped, and it explained a lot. His mother must have known how itsy-bitsy small his penis was, so maybe that's why she insisted he have a nice house. And maybe his dad has a small penis, too, and felt guilty for passing the little prick gene on. Like many men with small penises, he tried to make up for it with a Porsche. Most important, maybe he was afraid that if we did do it and got married, I would never know what a regular-size penis felt like, which really is quite considerate when you think about it. Or maybe he just really needed to focus on studying, and if boning me wasn't in the immediate future, he didn't want to deal with it. One thing I did know was that was the last time I would ever tell a guy I was a virgin.

Soon afterward, I started dating Ned. He had been on the soap opera *Santa Barbara* for years, but the show had gone off the air. He was tall for an actor and pretty good-looking, not perfection but very appealing. I gave him my number at an art/ free appetizers/DJ playing party. When he called a few days later, he said, "You don't know what I went through to find your number that I accidentally threw away. Let's just say it was pretty disgusting." Ned was funny and had bought a house when he was on the soap, which he now rented out at a profit. He rented another house with a roommate. I was impressed with his business sense for an actor and he was always busy auditioning.

I had sworn off guys in the entertainment business after I went on one date with an alternative stand-up comic, right before Ned. He said he hated the beach. At first I didn't believe him and thought he was just saying that to fit into the grungy Janeane Garofalo alternative comedy scene, which was about hating everything conventional. But again, who hates the beach? I pressed him on the subject and asked what if it was Hawaii, the Four Seasons, all expenses paid—but no, he said he hated the beach. I thought to myself as I finished my penne pasta arrabiata, no honeymoon on the beach, no taking the kids to the beach club to build sand castles—yep, this date is over! I was home by nine-thirty and pissed because the date with the beach hater was on Valentine's Day. After accepting his invitation, a doctor I had been out with once asked me to a dinner party with other doctors on Valentine's Day, too. I chose to go with the beach hater because he had asked me first and I figured God would reward me for keeping my word, which He didn't.

When the big night came, the beach hater hadn't even made reservations because he claimed he didn't know it was Valentine's Day. For good measure, he added that he didn't believe in it, either, something about how it's just another way for the corrupt corporations and the greeting card industry to profit off a made-up holiday. I tried to explain that Saint Valentine was a real saint, but it didn't seem to matter. Sadly, we ended up at the Olive Garden. I hate it when I have two sets of plans to choose from and choose the wrong one.

Ned, however, loved the beach, which was fitting since he was on a soap. In describing him to my friends, Ned was soon referred to as "Santa Barbara." Everyone I dated past or present had a descriptive name: "Beach Hater," "Divorced Dad," "Hand Model," and now "Thimble Dick." After dating for a few weeks and blue balling Santa Barbara numerous times, I decided to go on the pill, take it for a month so that it was in full effect, and then bone Ned one night without any big virginity speech. He didn't have to know.

Santa Barbara told me that his ex-girlfriend, a swimsuit model who he had lived with, just tried to kill herself and her mom called him to come over. This happened to be the Fourth of July weekend, which really pissed me off because I wanted to have a good Fourth of July and spend it with someone I cared about. What was up with my love life getting killed on holidays?

The year before, Derek, a guy whom I had dated once, invited me to meet him in San Diego, where we would spend the Fourth of July on his friend's boat. I had my sister Shannon join me. Shannon was always the best person to bring to a thing like this. She's blonde and pretty, really easygoing, and most important, nice. So even if she was not interested in my guy's friends, she would drink, laugh, and make out with one of them, anyway. My friend Tara, in contrast, was the worst. One time, I introduced her to my guy's friend who had been playing volleyball all day and drinking all night, and she looked straight at me in front of him and said, "Is this a joke? Look how red his face is. Heather, absolutely no!" I had to lie to him and say that she wasn't a coldhearted bitch but rather had recently lost a relative to skin cancer and never wanted to experience that pain again. I then lectured him about the importance of sunscreen.

When Shannon and I reached San Diego, we checked into a hotel room and met Derek and his friends at a bar. It was fun, but I knew I was not that into Derek. At least we'd have an amazing day on the boat. The next morning, Derek called. I thought it was to tell us where to meet at the dock, but instead he said, "I've got good news and bad news. The good news is, it's an amazing day; the bad news is my friend had an emergency back in Arizona where he lives and never made it out here with his boat." I was silent for about a minute until I said, "Are you kidding me? The boat is the only reason I came to San Diego." Shannon couldn't believe how awful I was being, but I really wanted to have a good Fourth of July. She convinced me to make the best of it, which was difficult.

We ended up meeting Derek at his friend's apartment near one of the universities. We packed cans of beer—not even light beer, so I knew I would be completely bloated in my bikini—in backpacks and walked about a mile to the crowded public beach, where we drank the warm high-caloric beers. I had planned on sipping champagne while heavily accessorized in my bikini and heels à la Puff Daddy, J Lo style. Instead, I was buzzed and full while reading people's neck tattoos.

When I found out for the second year in a row that my Fourth of July plans were being changed at the last minute, I got pissed. I told Santa Barbara, "If you two are broken up and don't plan on getting back together, do you really think seeing her is a good idea?" He said he felt he had to try to help her. I felt that pushing him to wait until the fifth of July so that we could attend my friend's shindig in the Palisades might make me look a tad insensitive, so I let it go.

Now that I didn't have Santa Barbara with me, I questioned not going to the married couples' party and instead going to a Groundling's party in Los Feliz. I couldn't do both. You have to choose one party on the Fourth of July, especially if one is at the beach and one is in the Hollywood Hills. With traffic it could take two hours, and nothing is more depressing than seeing fireworks go off when you're still en route, trying to poke your head out of your window to see them while stuck at a red light. Good luck finding the radio station playing *The Star Spangled Banner* so that you can sing along. I finally decided to stick with the Palisades party. It was pleasant, good drinks, kids in the pool, but no potential guys for me unless I was willing to break up a marriage and become an insta-stepmother.

The next day, I found out I had made a monumental mistake. I chose the wrong party. I had made the wrong plans yet again! The Los Feliz Groundlings' party was packed with *Saturday Night Live* cast members, hip stand-up comics, and up-and-coming industry types. Shit, I was pissed. The previous Groundlings/*Saturday Night Live* cast member party was at a Hollywood apartment building, and I made out with Will Ferrell in the community pool. Sure, he tried to get away, but I'm an excellent swimmer and took first place in the breast stroke when I was six years old, so I managed to get a few more kisses in. I would have never bothered in the past, but he had already done a full season on *Saturday Night Live,* so he was instantly more attractive. The eight Corona Lights didn't hurt, either. Who knows what could have happened at this party? Maybe I could have actually met someone who could have put me on *SNL* instead of just putting my tongue in a cast member's mouth.

Santa Barbara called me during the week and said his ex was doing better but that he stayed there all night on the couch. I didn't know what to think. The guy I'm about to lose my virginity to is stuck in some sick codependent relationship with a suicidal supermodel. We attempted to make plans midweek, but then he remembered he had "something." We made plans to go out Saturday night. I didn't hear from him on Wednesday or Thursday, so I called him Friday and tried to sound all casual. "Oh, hey, it's Heather. Hope you had a good week. I'm sorry I haven't talked to you—I've been *soooo* busy. Looking forward to seeing you Saturday. Call me." I didn't hear from him Friday night, either.

Saturday morning, instead of looking forward to my date, I started to wonder if he was going to cancel. I put on my light blue biking shorts and matching sports bra and walked down to Whole Foods. I checked my voice mail from the store—

nothing. When I came home, I checked it again—nothing. I called a girlfriend and gave her the lowdown and we tried to decipher what it might mean.

As the sun began to set, I could not believe I had been stood up. My mother told me a story about when she was stood up for some ball in college. She got all dressed up and waited and waited. The next day, she saw the guy and decided to act like nothing had happened.

"Why didn't you say, 'Hey asshole, I got a dress and did my hair and you didn't show up. What happened?'"

My mother said, "No, I didn't want him to know he hurt me."

She also told me never to order ribs on a date. The ribs I agreed with but not her philosophy about not letting the guy know he hurt you.

So I came up with a plan. Earlier that day, a passenger plane went down. It was horrible. I knew he wasn't on it, but I just had to get him to call me back. So I called him up around nine p.m. and said, "I'm sorry I'm just calling now. I thought I knew someone on that plane and then I realized I never heard from you and we had plans. I hope and pray you did not know anyone on that plane. Please let me know you and your loved one are OK." OK, that was a horrible lie. Believe me, after I hung up, I knew every nun, priest, and karma-preaching yoga instructor would have been appalled, but I was desperate.

Sure enough, he called the next day and said, "Hey, um, wow, you thought you knew someone on the flight? Hope everything is OK. I, ah, I laid down around seven and I fell asleep. Yeah, I fell asleep. Sorry. Call me."

That's all I needed. He could have gotten laid that night by a virgin but instead decided to stand me up. He called me twice after that, but I did not return his calls. This out-of-work soap star was not worthy of the Heather McDonald cherry pop. I don't know if he was frustrated waiting for me to put out and said forget it or if the suicidal swimsuit model got a new prescription and they got back together. All I know is that I've only seen him in one commercial and one guest spot since, and I watch a lot of TV, so he's not exactly setting the world on fire. Knock on wood, I haven't been in a plane crash yet, either, but it is a dream of mine to survive one solely because of my excellent swimming skills.

After the Santa Barbara debacle, I decided to join Great Expectations. It should have been called Lowered Expectations. Great Expectations was a dating service. Unlike the online dating services today, Great Expectations predated cyberspace and was supposed to be the best singles bar ever. It was also very expensive. They videotaped every member, so along with personal profiles, a prospective suitor could see how you acted and spoke on video before deciding to go on a date with you. It cost over two thousand dollars to join. My parents and my friends thought I was crazy for wanting to do this at the age of twenty-five. But that was exactly why I wanted to do it. I explained, "I want to get married and have kids, and I don't want to wake up at thirty in a panic. I want to start weeding out people and only date men who fit my criteria and want to get married." I also thought it would lend to stand-up material and new characters for me at The Groundlings. I planned to watch videos of some of the dorky women and later impersonate them in a sketch. But to my dismay, I learned after joining that I was only allowed to view videos of the opposite sex. I guess they didn't have a gay division yet.

A week after joining and recording my video, I went into the Great Expectations offices to see if anyone had chosen me. To my surprise, eighty-four guys had. Even though my profile stated that I was looking for tall, educated, attractive men between the ages of twenty-five and forty, I seemed to get a little of everything. I was supposed to look up each guy's profile to see if it interested me, then find his video and watch it. Their filing system was more difficult than the Dewey decimal system used by public libraries. After spending hours rejecting ugly, boring people, I began to actually answer the question as to why I was rejecting them in a multiple-choice checklist. I'd check age if they were eligible for their AARP card, I'd check religion if they were Muslim, and I'd check education if they never went to college. Then the rejected suitor had the option of sending me a letter through Great Expectations. Some of those letters were nice, but some were downright nasty.

One read: "Heather, I saw your profile and you said you were Catholic so I thought youd [sic] be nice but instead your [sic] mean. You said you didn't chose [sic] me because of education. Well, I find that colege [sic] people are some of the most meanestest [sic] people out there. You're un-christian [sic] like and just a big meenie [sic] and your [sic] not even that preetty [sic]." Need I comment on that one?

The next day, I walked in and told the woman at the desk

who informed me that another 104 men requested me that I was totally overwhelmed and needed to quit. I guess no decent-looking twenty-five-year-old woman had ever joined. It was as if I was Megan Fox and had suddenly posted a profile. I asked the receptionist, who was attractive and had a sense of style, "Look, I can't research all these people. Look at me. Is there anyone on this list I would be interested in?" She looked at all 104 names and circled two. I then automatically rejected the other 102 by checking "conflict of hobbies" just to get through it quickly.

I imagined some rejected suitors were confused, thinking who has that strong of an aversion to stamp collecting? I went to look up the two guys she recommended, which took me a good twenty minutes to find. The first one was twenty-nine, in sales, and looked pretty cute. But in his profile he wrote that he was a very devout Mormon and always gave at least 10 percent of his gross salary to the Church of Latter Day Saints. I was more bothered by the amount of money he was giving away than the possibility of one day having a sister wife, even though it would be nice to have someone help milk the cows and tend to all the children. I rejected him based on overgenerosity.

I had once gone out with a Jewish lawyer who was hot and fun, but on our third date we went into a pizza joint and I suggested getting the Hawaiian pizza. Granted, it's a pretty disgusting pizza with ham and pineapple, but I had always loved it. He said, "I can't get that."

And I said, "I know a lot of people are grossed out by the pineapple with tomato sauce."

He replied, "No, because of the ham. I keep kosher."

"Like you have two dishwashers and two refrigerators in your home at all times, that kind of keeping kosher?"

"Yes, I do." After finishing my piece of vegetarian cheese pizza, I knew I'd never see him again. Jewish is one thing, but keeping kosher is just too Jewish for me. A guy who keeps kosher is going to want to marry a Jewish girl or one who would convert. The last thing I wanted to do after twelve years of Catholic school was take a bunch of classes and tests on a whole new religion.

The other guy was Victor. In his picture, he was standing in between a man and woman with his arms around them, wearing a nice black trench coat and—bonus—he was taller than both of them. Then I read his occupation: Orthopedist. Oh my God, he's a doctor! I continued to read as my heart began to beat a little faster. He was thirty-seven, not bad, only twelve years older than me, no kids, never been married, and then the icing on the cake, religion: Catholic. I told myself that this has got to be too good to be true. I filled out the card, allowing the service to give Dr. Victor my phone number. Within hours, my phone rang and it was Dr. Victor calling from an airport. My first thought was, Wow, this doctor is really eager to meet me—so much that he couldn't wait to get home to call me. Maybe it's because we are meant to be together. We made plans for him to pick me up at my house a few days later. I was now renting a place with my sister and another girl, Susan. It was in Brentwood and a stone's throw away from the O.J. Simpson crime scene. Even though it took place years earlier, people still parked in front of our house to walk across the street and take pictures.

Dr. Victor arrived on time in a brand-new Porsche, which really blew the doors off Jason's old, tired Porschette. I felt like it was a good sign. We went to the Hollywood Bowl, where he had box seats, and we drank wine, talked, and danced. The date could not have gone better. So what did it matter that Great Expectations was a bunch of unattractive desperate losers? Neither of us were, and we found each other. It only takes meeting one person, if it's the right person, to last a lifetime, and the two thousand plus dollars I spent would be more than worth it.

Dr. Victor and I had a lot in common. For example, he had no desire to ever go camping, and neither did I. Dr. Victor was smart, of course, but not an intellectual snob by any means. We joked about what to tell people about how we met, since neither of us wanted to admit it was through Great Expectations. For some reason, I liked telling people that he approached me at the self-service gas pump while I was filling my tank. He didn't like that, probably because it sounded like something sleazy that would happen at a truck stop.

On our third date, I went to his house in Hermosa Beach, a few blocks from the water. He admitted to hiring a decorator, who had done the place in a Southwestern theme, with cactus statues everywhere and a color scheme of mint, light peach, and cream. It was pretty tacky, but that is what a new wife is for—to redecorate, right? All day, he kept saying he had a surprise for me. So far, surprises from the men in my life had been pretty disappointing, and this was no exception. He had two tickets to go to the Comedy and Magic Club in Hermosa Beach.

The last thing I wanted to do was sit in the audience at a

comedy club on my one night off from doing stand-up. But he thought he was being really thoughtful. Some guys thought my comedy aspirations were futile or that they were in fact funnier than me, which was seriously annoying. Other times, they were overly into it, wanting to see me perform all the time, asking questions about it, or worse, admitting that they, too, wanted to be a stand-up. This wasn't totally a bad sign for Dr. Victor, so I just told him that I was tired, and we watched *Fatal Attraction,* which is hands down my favorite movie. I know it's not the most appropriate film to watch with someone you are newly dating, since Glenn Close goes crazy, boils a rabbit, and wields a knife, but I didn't care. Besides the fact that I love the classic film genre of infidelity, there's her New York white apartment and lines like, "I'm not going to be ignored, Dan." Thankfully, it didn't seem to freak Dr. Victor out that I was obsessed with a movie about a female stalker—and that I acted out the scenes verbatim—another gold star for him.

Prior to meeting Dr. Victor, my sister Shannon, our roommate Susan, and I planned on having a housewarming party, since we had just moved in. I had no intention of inviting Dr. Victor. The thought of having to introduce him to all of my friends as just someone I was dating (we weren't exclusive or anything) was not something I wanted to do. He wouldn't know anyone, so I'd have to babysit him. Besides, there would be no chance of me meeting or hooking up with anyone else, so I just didn't mention it. But a stupid friend of mine who knew a friend of his did.

This wasn't the first time I'd gotten in trouble for not inviting people to parties. There was the time the booker of a stand-up room inside a topless strip club got all offended that I didn't invite him to my birthday party. Since he was disgusting and tried to convince me to audition for amateur night on the main stage where the chicken wings were served after my ten-minute stand-up set in the smaller peep show room, I didn't feel our relationship called for an invitation to my birthday party. To get me back, he stopped booking me at the very prestigious "Fantasy Island." I felt the same about Dr. Victor. Having him there would stress me out, and I wanted to hang out with my college and Groundlings friends. I tried to explain it to him and that he wasn't missing anything, but it was difficult to hear him over the blaring music and laughter in my house when he called.

Before our next date, as I applied my lip liner, I had what Oprah would call an "aha" moment. I did not want to go. I just wasn't into him. He was great on paper, but the initial excitement had worn off. After dinner, he brought me home and we kissed a little on my bed, and I was so not into it that I pretended to fall asleep, so he eventually left.

Shortly afterward, he threw out his back and was all annoyed that I didn't offer to come over and make him soup and play nurse. Again with the soup! He told me he had an upcoming surgery for a deviated septum, which in layman's terms means "Hello, nose job." I was a little creeped out that a thirty-seven-year-old man was into plastic surgery, especially since he also divulged that while he was under he was going to get liposuction on his love handles. Maybe because he was an orthopedist, he struck some deal with the plastic surgeon to swap services. His nose was better than mine to begin with. I've always had a bump on my nose, and around this time, I was working in real estate. I was showing one of our listings to a doctor who was known for doing the "lunchtime nose job." At the end of the showing, he got really close to me and whispered, "So when are you going to call me?" I was appalled because he was married and his wife was literally within earshot of us, so I said, "Doctor, I am flattered, but I don't date clients and certainly not married ones." He said, "No, I meant for your nose. From the moment I met you, I've been dying to get you in my office and straighten out your bridge." Now, if I was able to get past that humiliation and live with the imperfect schnoz God blessed me with, why couldn't he?

In my sorority, during a chapter meeting, three of our members from the same high school all turned to the side at the same time to look at something, and they all had the exact same nose. It was freaky, like a *Twilight Zone* episode. Obviously, they all went to the same local plastic surgeon, but it made a strong impression on me. Also, there can be so many ramifications. Like when two contestants from the TV show *The Swan,* where they have multiple plastic surgeries, met, fell in love, and procreated. They looked all cute with their turned-up noses, and their baby came out looking like a bald fifty-year-old accountant. It was all just too much. I decided to stop calling Dr. Victor back, figuring he'd see the writing on the wall. But he didn't get it. Instead, he called every day for two weeks straight, leaving me messages like everything was great between us.

"Hi Heather, it's Victor. I'm still recovering from my surgery, but after the bandages come off, I want to take you to dinner. Call me. My office is . . . my home is . . . my cell is . . . my pager is . . . my fax is . . ." One day I walked in on him leaving yet another message on my answering machine, and this time it was different. After weeks of not returning his calls, he said, "Heather, I hate to do this on an answering machine, but I don't think it's going to work out between us."

I yelled back at the machine "Oh, ya don't! Why? Because I haven't called you back after fourteen messages. Nothing gets past you!"

He continued leaving his message: "To be perfectly honest, I think you are a little immature for me and quite selfish. The fact that I not only threw my back out but underwent two surgeries and you still failed to provide any comfort for me was a real turnoff. I think you are selfish and a bit snobbish." As I was listening to this, I couldn't believe that a man his age had still not learned proper voice-mail etiquette, which is to never leave a message you may later regret. So before Dr. Victor could do some serious damage, I picked up the phone and said, "Victor, it's Heather."

"Oh hi, Heather. How are you?" he asked very nicely.

I then answered, "I guess snobby, selfish, immature, the list just goes on, doesn't it . . ."

He interrupted. "No, I just meant . . . I don't know what happened. Everything was going so great, and there was that night when you clearly wanted me and I could have done whatever I wanted to you, but I was a gentleman and left."

"You could have done anything you wanted to me if you

were a rapist. I fell asleep," I clarified. "Look, you clearly don't get hints. I fell asleep because I didn't want to have sex with you, and I never returned your calls because, let's see, I didn't want to talk to you," I yelled.

"Fine, well good luck to you then," he said.

"Well, good luck to you, your nose, and new svelte middle section," I replied and hung up.

Fortunately, I never heard from or ran into Dr. Victor again. Even though I never set foot in the offices of Great Expectations ever again, it continued to haunt me in the form of letters from rejectees asking me to please reconsider going out with them. Or a few times a strange man would approach me at Starbucks or at Coffee Bean and Tea Leaf and ask, "Are you Heather?" At first, I'd get excited, thinking it was a Groundlings fan or a potential real estate client who was familiar with my face on the bus benches. Then I'd realize from the weird look in his eyes that it was from Great Expectations, and I'd have to quickly think on my feet. Thanks to all my improvisational training, I once said, "Oh, I'm sorry. I'm not Heather." Just then, the barista yelled, "Nonfat vanilla latte for Heather!"

Finally, I called Great Expectations, and even though I had more than two years on my three-year contract left, I insisted that they cancel my membership and remove me from the books, the videos, and the archives. Everyone was right, after all. It was stupid and a waste of money to join this dating service. I guess I had to experience it for myself. Nowadays, online dating is a much better option, but I don't think I could even figure out how to upload my cute pictures onto a site.

 Conversations with Ben

B en and I met at a Starbucks as many unemployed people do. I was just fired from my first television writing job. It was pilot season. In the entertainment industry, this means that they're casting for possible new TV shows. I had an audition for the role of—once again—the best friend of the lead in a sitcom about twenty-somethings struggling in LA. I had never called in sick during the eleven weeks I worked as a writer, so I did this one time. What's the harm, I thought. No one is going to know I'm auditioning. That morning, I woke up, called the assistant, got his voice mail, coughed a few times, and made my voice sound as Demi Moore-ish as possible. "Hi, it's Heather. I'm really sick. [sniffle sound] I don't know what it is. I'm so sorry [and then I faked a cough that sounded like an oyster just popped out of my throat]. I can't come in today. Please tell everyone."

As I always did for auditions, I had prepared myself well for all three of the unfunny scenes with the role of Missy. Missy was Carol's best friend and worked in shipping and receiving at a plastics plant. If it wasn't for Missy's tabby-colored cat, Mr. Peepers, Missy would spend most Saturday nights alone. But after realizing that she's not getting any younger, Missy decides to comb the personal ads for her Prince Charming.

I was excited to read for the role of Missy because she was described as "attractive." Now, "attractive" I could handle. "Extremely attractive," I didn't have a shot in hell of getting. If the role was described as "a character," I knew I'd be the cutest one in the casting director's waiting room.

I arrived in the cramped waiting room of one of the trailers on the studio lot. The assistant casting director, who looked about twelve, came out with a clipboard and said, "The casting director had to leave for an emergency. Her King Charles cocker spaniel got diarrhea at doggy daycare, so you guys will be reading with me instead. Oh, and we're only doing the first scene." Suddenly, all the actresses were kissing this middle-school girl's ass, saying, "Oh my God! What happened to her doggie? My sister has a King Charles puppy and he needs a hip replacement. . . ."

The only thing more uninteresting than hearing the details of dog surgery is hearing the details of human surgery. And the only thing better than that is any story about a slipped disc. Didn't these idiots get it? None of us were even in the running anymore. The part was most likely already cast. Oh well. At least I still had my writing job, or so I thought.

That night I got a call from the assistant at the TV show where I worked saying that I could pick up my things tomorrow and that I was no longer needed. I felt like such an idiot, but I tried to look on the bright side. It was pilot season and maybe I'd get to go on another sitcom audition that I'd waste all day preparing for and never get. Besides, writing on the TV show allowed me very little time to date, so it was for the best that I got fired. For some God-forsaken reason, we couldn't leave until after ten p.m. every night, even though we weren't working on anything. I'd be so burned out by the thirteen-hour days that by the time the weekend came, all I'd do was lay in my bed and watch episodes of Jerry Springer. It made me feel better that even though I didn't have a man, at least I had teeth. I later found out that when the executive producer asked the assistant where I was, before he could even answer, one of the bitter, overweight, baseball hat–wearing, single forty-year-old male comedy writers said, "Well, you know where she is. It's pilot season." Thanks for throwing me under the bus, dickwad. No wonder the only woman he could get to accompany him to the Christmas party was a Russian hooker named Pineapple.

I had some money saved, so I decided to write a script in between all the auditions that would come my way. My plan was to either book a sitcom or sell a script, whichever came first. How exciting! I imagined my script as a female-driven romantic comedy. After Julia Roberts got her hands on it, a bidding war would break out with Cameron Diaz because they'd both be dying to play the role of the hilarious, clumsy, type-A prosecutor who can't find love until she meets him in the courtroom. He, of course, is the defense attorney opposite her on the biggest case of her life. Now, I can be a sellout. However, in my big-budget romantic comedy, I have to draw the line at the female lead running on a treadmill, being distracted by a cute guy, causing her to stop running, and thus falling out of frame. I do have some comedy morals, and if I see that scene one more time, I'm going to fall out of frame and kill myself.

So on my first day of being an unemployed actress/screenwriter, I decided to take the pilot sitcom script for which I had an audition the following day to the Starbucks closest to my house on the corner of 7th and San Vicente in Santa Monica. It was a beautiful March day, a sunny, breezy 77 degrees. I put on my Lycra yoga pants and sports bra, since I would be walking an entire two blocks to get there, so I obviously needed the proper attire in case I was to break a sweat. I spent twenty-five minutes doing my hair and makeup. I never left the house without makeup, because I read in *Cosmo* that you never know where you might meet your future husband, so always look your best including your run to Starbucks. I put my yellow highlighter, lip gloss, and five dollars in my butt pack (yes, I wore a black butt pack; they are extremely convenient when wearing clothes void of pockets), grabbed the script, and began the first day of the rest of my life at approximately ten-fifteen a.m.

I ordered my usual double-tall nonfat latte with one and a half Equals and a bran muffin and took a table outside. This time of the morning was too late for the workforce as well as the stay-at-home moms, who have to leave Starbucks by nine-fifteen to make their spinning classes, but it was still too early for the homeless people, so it was quite sparse. I felt great pride in finding my character's name in the script and highlighting each and every one of her lines. I was extremely self-conscious. How can you not be at a Starbucks? I hoped people noticed I had a real script here, something that had been green lit and would be shot, though most likely it would never be broadcast. But still, I was in the mix people, and I wasn't some poseur fresh from a Learning Annex class.

I had my earphones in and was listening to Sade and doing what I always do when I hear any Sade song. I imagined myself hosting a party at a Tuscan retreat in Malibu wearing a loose white linen ankle-length dress while carrying a huge goblet of cold Chardonnay and walking around my blue-tiled infinity pool greeting all of my guests with light touches to their shoulders and friendly giggles. Just then, the coffee and the bran muffin kicked in.

This combo never fails. When I got up to go to the bathroom, I noticed a really sexy guy talking to a woman. We clearly had eye contact as he completely checked me and my butt pack out as I walked right past him. Another reason I liked the butt pack was that it cut the length of my long flat ass in half, making it appear shorter and more pronounced. Upon returning from the bathroom a pound and a half lighter, I had direct eye contact again with the sexy Starbucks stranger and he smirked at me. He had a great smirk. I politely smiled back, sat down, put my ear phones back in, and continued to memorize my snarky remarks like, "His personal ad read entrepreneur [I practiced saying entrepreneur in finger quotes]. In case you didn't know, that's French for unemployed [finger quotes again, hilarious]. . . ."

By noon, the smirking stranger was still there talking to the woman, who appeared to be a platonic friend. He was casually dressed but still hip and stylish. I took out my earphones just as the woman he was with got up to go to the bathroom.

"What script are you reading?" he asked.

"Oh, it's for an audition I have tomorrow, for a really funny new show on the WB," I said proudly.

He was really good-looking. I could see between his wrist-watch and his shirt cuff that he was tattooed, but not just a tattoo, the kind of tattoo that is multicolored and all smashed to-gether. He was "sleeved" as they like to call it in the tattoo biz. I don't have a tattoo and have never had the desire to get one, but on certain guys they can be really attractive in a bad boy kind of way. He had a New York City accent, which has always turned me on. I don't like English or country, only New York City. Along with the tattoos, he smoked. I've never smoked nor dated a smoker, but something about him smoking was again just sexy and it went with his whole persona. Think Mickey Rourke. Not Mickey Rourke from *The Wrestler* with the cheek implants, face-lift, and bizarre outfit, but old school Mickey Rourke from the movie *9 1/2 Weeks,* where he manipulated the crap out of Kim Basinger, blindfolded her, and fed her a shit load of food and then made her dress up like a man complete with a fake mus-tache. He kind of had that same vibe. I could also sense he had the way New York men take care of everything for you kind of attitude that you don't see in guys from other cities. New Jersey was like this, too. Like Tony Soprano, although he was a bald, fat criminal, he was also caring, protective, and sexy.

I told him that besides being an actress, I was also a writer. He seemed impressed, as he should have been. Just then, his female companion returned. He introduced himself as Ben and the woman as his assistant, Susan.

"What do you do?" I asked.

"I'm a stockbroker and investment banker," he replied.

This being 1998, the stock market was very good and on the rise. It was the dot-com boom, where the words *Internet start-up company* could make gold diggers this side of Silicon Valley cum in an instant.

"Where is your office?" I asked.

"Actually, right now I'm able to work out of my home, which is right across from the water. We were just taking a little break, since we start at six in the morning when the stock market opens in New York."

"That must be nice. I live just down the street and I love it," I replied.

"You are adorable, you know that? Isn't she adorable?" he said to his assistant. "Look, she's blushing," he continued. It was physically impossible to keep my cheeks from not getting red. "Can I take you to dinner one night this week?"

Absolutely, I thought. I loved his confidence, but instead I said, "Um, sure, I think." As I wrote down my number on the last page of the sitcom script and tore it off, I acted as though I was reluctant about it. This in turn made him feel like he had accomplished something, which was my total intention. He and his assistant stood up to leave, and he said, "I'm going to call you." He pointed at me and winked.

"OK." I said feeling like I had accomplished something. If my girlfriends and I went out to a bar or a party and I didn't at least give out my number, I felt like it was a wasted night. Here it was a Thursday before noon and I already gave out my number. This unemployment thing was really working out.

A couple minutes after they left, another woman said to me, "Excuse me, but did you happen to hear what that guy and that woman were talking about before you gave your number to him?"

"No, I had my earphones in the whole time," I said.

"Well, I don't mean to intrude, but you should not go out with him. They were talking about how he might have to do time in jail," she added.

"Oh my God. Well, thanks. I doubt he'll call, anyway," I said.

"Well, in case he does, I'd watch out."

Wow, way to watch a fellow Starbucks' sister's back, strange lady. Too bad I didn't watch out.

I really didn't think Ben would call, so I was surprised when I heard his voice-mail message. I was creeped out hearing about his possible jail incarceration but also intrigued. At the time, I went out with a lot of guys just for the sake of a two-course meal. I didn't judge a guy so much on what he did for a living but more on what was in his wallet. If I wanted an appetizer before my entrée, it couldn't be a big issue. Either he had to accept that I was having a salad before my shrimp scampi or we couldn't see each other again. Ben said he wanted to take me to Ocean, a very nice hip seafood restaurant, on Tuesday night. I thought, Why not go? If I can have lobster tail for free versus Panda Express for $6.99, why wouldn't I take full advantage of it? It just made fiscal sense to go on this date.

At seven-thirty on Tuesday night, Ben called from downstairs to say he was in the lobby. I told him I'd be right down. I didn't feel the need for him to come up. Besides, the apartment was a disaster as usual. As I walked out the lobby doors, he was sitting in a white Infinity sedan smoking with all four windows rolled down, the sunroof open, and Verve blasting, "It's a bittersweet symphony that life . . ." It was so loud that I had to get all the way up to the car for him to notice me. He immediately got out of the car wearing a very expensive-looking tan suede blazer over a white T-shirt and designer jeans and opened my door for me, which I so loved.

Before we ordered drinks, he told me he didn't drink. I asked, "Like you never drank or you're in AA?"

"I'm in AA. I've been sober for nineteen months."

Wow, I had never dated an alcoholic before. Well, I had dated many alcoholics, but they were still drinking, which made it OK. I had never dated someone in "the program." Does this mean I can't drink on this date, either? I wondered. Lobster is not going to be as tasty with an ice tea unless that ice tea is from Long Island.

"Well, that's great. Good for you. Do you mind if I drink?" I asked.

"No, of course not," he said. What I've found is sober guys

are just as eager to get a girl drunk as drunk guys—maybe even more so. He also went on to say he was a heroin addict, too! OK, what am I doing? I thought. This guy smokes, has tattoos, is in AA and Narcotics Anonymous, and maybe going to jail. Is the free shellfish really worth it?

The closest I ever came to dating an addict of any kind was when I went to a Gamblers Anonymous meeting to see my friend Mike get his six-month chip. I always referred to Mike as "the bitter comic" (because he was a stand-up comic and was extremely bitter). When the meeting concluded, Bitter Comic said his friend wanted to take me out. When I said I wasn't interested, Bitter Comic said, "But he was in the NBA, he likes tall girls."

"Who cares that he *was* in the NBA? He just said he was a hundred and eighty thousand dollars in debt, rents a room from his grandmother, and his only means of transportation is a beach cruiser. What am I supposed to do, hop on the handle bars and hope for the best?" Bitter Comic later said the NBA player said I was a bitch for not giving him a chance. I suggested that the next time he sees a tall girl he is attracted to at a GA meeting he should refrain from participating in share time.

But with Ben I was more intrigued than ever.

Ben was so addicted to smoking that he had to get up twice to light up because you can't smoke in restaurants in LA; then toward the end of the night, he lit up right at the table and hid it. All the while, I kept telling him how much I didn't mind the smoke in between wiping tears from my irritated eyes and attempting not to cough. After a few martinis, I related what the woman at Starbucks told me about him discussing jail. He told me that he was very successful in New York and there was some mix-up with some stock tip, and basically it's a white-collar crime, but if he did go to jail, it would only be for eight months to a year at the most, but he wouldn't know for sure until his court date, which was still a few more months away. Phew, I mean it wasn't like I was dating John Gotti. I had to give him credit for being honest, right? Google did not exist then and I wasn't about to take the time to find a library, do all the paperwork to get a library card, and go through microfiche like Debra Winger in the movie *Black Widow*. It's just a total stranger who picked me up in his car and took me to dinner. What could possibly happen? It wasn't like I was going to fall in love with him. He was just fun.

The most attractive thing about Ben was how wonderful he thought I was. Finally, someone got it. He considered himself very spiritual and had read every popular soul-searching self-help book at the time. He presented me with *Conversations with God,* a book about conversations the author claims to have had with God, where God actually answered back. Inside the cover, Ben wrote me this incredible inscription with all these compliments that I had never been told before, probably because they weren't true. The note was all about how intelligent and intuitive I was. Again, I was thinking, Finally, a guy who really gets the real me. He also recommended such books as *The Artist's Way* and anything Marianne Williamson wrote. Williamson was Oprah's Dr. Oz of the late nineties. She was on the show all the time, and then one day Oprah just never had her back. Good thing Dr. Oz got his own show out of it. Though I have always been Catholic and truly never explored any other religions, for some reason I always get approached to join other churches.

In college, we had this big Christian speaker who was just named "Josh." Prior to his arrival, there were big signs all over campus that only read: "Josh is coming." I was like, who the hell is Josh, so I went. He was a very dynamic Christian speaker and I enjoyed what he had to say, but that was it. Later, a few other students who saw me there kept going out of their way to invite me to other things involving their Christian church, which I always politely turned down. One night I was walking to the library and I passed the Sigma Alpha Epsilon house. One of the guys, Jeff, who spotted me at "Josh" and who I knew from my communications class, asked if I'd like to come to a Bible study they were having there in a few minutes. I said, "Oh thank you, but I have to go to the library." Then a girl approached with her Bible and Jeff said, "Sarah, this is Heather. She heard Josh speak. She's going to join us tonight for Bible study."

I tried to correct him. "Actually, I have to get to the library. . . ."

Sarah cut me off. "Oh, that's great. We have a special guest tonight. You're going to love it."

"Oh, I can't come. I have a paper on the fall of Rome and it has to be no less than forty pages single spaced, and I haven't started it yet and it's due tomorrow."

Then Jeff said, "Isn't it great that Heather is going to join us tonight?"

I said again, "I wish I could, but I'm really behind. I have another paper on *War and Peace,* and it's ninety percent of our grade and I haven't even checked out the book yet, so I need to go to the library and start reading."

Then Sarah said, "Tonight we are going to be studying some passages from the Book of John."

Was everyone deaf? Was I in the Twilight Zone? Why was no one hearing me say, "No!" The Christians must teach some incredible sales techniques. No wonder so many of them are successful in business.

I tried again. "I can't come tonight."

Then Jeff said, "We are so excited to have you join us tonight."

Now I was getting annoyed. Finally, I just said, "I'm Catholic. We don't study the Bible. Sorry." I practically started running with my heavy backpack bouncing up and down my back. As cute as that Sigma Alpha Epsilon was, I avoided him for the rest of the blessed Christian semester.

Growing up, we lived within a mile of a Jehovah Witness Kingdom Hall. They would always knock on our door and my parents taught us to say, "No, thank you. We're Catholic." Sometimes they would say, "OK," but oftentimes they would say, "Well, please take our literature. It's about building a stronger family." I always felt so bad for them; still do. Walking door-to-door in the heat, does anyone really just join a church because someone knocks on their door and asks them to? I guess some must; otherwise, they would stop doing it.

Over the years, I was continuously approached and invited to other Christian churches. Catholics never recruit anyone because they don't have to. Catholics don't get excited when you show up, but they do get annoyed when you duck out early. They've trained generations to come on Sunday and bring a check, and that is why I'm a practicing Catholic today. I know the deal. It never changes and I like it like that. But when Ben handed me *Conversations with God,* I told him and myself that I was very open to other means of spirituality. I'd taken a few yoga classes and said "Namaste," which did make me feel like I was breaking the Third Commandment—"Thou shall not worship other gods"—until a friend explained to me what it actually meant.

I'm not the closed-minded Catholic I once was. Sometimes I even toyed with the idea of checking out Scientology. The lead in the hit sitcom *Dharma and Greg,* Jenna Elfman, is a Scientologist. That must have had something to do with her getting the part. How else could you explain a show about a hippie girl marrying a conservative guy lasting for five seasons? Maybe there was something that Scientologists could unlock in me so that I could actually book a role. It later occurred to me that lots of famous successful actors were Catholics, Jews, and Protestants—many more than Scientologists—so it was best to stick with what I knew and not rock the God boat.

I liked that Ben was in AA, too. When I first started stand-up, I considered going to an AA meeting, not because I was an alcoholic, but just because I felt I could really use the free stage time. I had also heard about a certain AA meeting on Robertson Boulevard in Beverly Hills that a lot of industry people went to. I fantasized about attending and possibly getting a recovering yet more powerful theatrical agent. Ben loved this meeting and often went to it. That is where, according to Ben, he met the female Miramax executive who wanted to make his life story into a major motion picture.

My first manager was in AA. His name was Eric. He saw me at the Comedy Store and told me to call him the next day, so I did. He told me to come by his office, which I did later that day. As I drove up, I thought his office looked more like an apartment building than an office building housing the goings-on of the entertainment industry. Well, it turned out it was his apartment. I knew this wasn't a good sign, but I was so excited to have someone—anyone, actually—want to represent me that I convinced myself that this way he could concentrate on my comedy career twenty-four hours a day. Just like Ben, Eric smoked cigarettes, drank a lot of Starbucks, and thought I was beyond wonderful. Unlike Ben, he was not attractive. He was bald even though he was only twenty-seven, had never visited an orthodontist, and was about thirty pounds overweight. One day, I couldn't get a hold of Eric, and when he called me back, he told me his phone was disconnected and he needed $180 to get it turned back on. Of course, I gave it to him. How else are all these casting directors and network executives going to get a hold of me?

Eric soon started calling me "baby girl" and wanted to see movies with me. I joined him, thinking we could talk about getting me some showcases at other comedy clubs during the previews. It didn't occur to me that Eric was interested in me sexually, because he was so much less attractive than me. But some guys, no matter what looks back at them in the mirror, think that as long as you take the time to talk to them, you also want to fuck them. So sure enough, with my $180 still withstanding, Eric leaned in to kiss me. As I pushed him away, I thought, Oh shit. Now I have to find a new manager, and does this mean I still have my spot at Igby's comedy club? I already invited a bunch of people from high school. I told him as politely as I could that I was only interested in him as a manager and he said he understood. He stopped returning my calls and was soon evicted from his apartment/entertainment management offices. Needless to say, I'm still waiting to be repaid the $180.

Ben and I started hanging out in the afternoons. He'd call me in the morning and we'd make plans to meet at Jamba Juice, which he always paid for. If we walked into any shop, he offered to buy me something, whether it was shampoo or clothing. If we were in a Barnes & Noble, he'd buy me more spiritual self-help books. The books were the only things I accepted. I didn't want to feel like I owed him anything. Because I was unemployed and he was doing whatever he claimed to be doing, we both had a lot of free time and were spending it together. He liked to do everything I liked to do: eating at fine restaurants, talking about me, watching my one-woman show on VHS over and over again, and making out. Since we'd only been seeing each other a week or two, he wasn't putting any pressure on me for sex, but I was really falling for him.

He was thirty-eight years old and had an incredible body. He told me all those years of doing heroin helped preserve his body. He also said how much he loved kids, and, of course, I've always loved kids and wanted to be a mother. We made plans for him to meet my sister Kathi and her two little girls for lunch on Montana Avenue in Santa Monica. I told my sister all about Ben and how fun, gorgeous, and cool he was. I did, however, leave out the rap sheet, and alcohol and heroin addictions. As we waited for Ben at the restaurant, I started to worry. It's not like him not to show up (not like him—I'd only known him ten days!), then he called my cell.

"What happened? Where are you?" I asked concerned.

"I'm really embarrassed. I don't have any cash on me for lunch." I thought that was strange, but before I could inquire anymore, he told some story about accidentally leaving his wallet with his AA sponsor the night before and the sponsor couldn't return it until later that day.

All I cared about was seeing Ben and for my sister to meet this sexy, hot, rich babe who was so into me. And at least he was going to his meetings, right?

"That's fine. I got it. Just come."

Ben came, and he and my sister hit it off. Walking back from the restaurant to his place, he put one of my nieces on his shoulders and could not be more charming as he invited my sister and her kids into his gorgeous three-bedroom apartment. My sister approved, of course.

A day or two later, he called me and said he went down to get his car and it was gone. I was shocked, because he lived in a beautiful complex overlooking the ocean with secured parking. How could his car have been stolen?

He said, "I need to rent a car in the meantime, but with my legal problems, my credit is shot."

I said, "But all you need is a valid credit card to get a rental car."

He responded, "I don't have a credit card. That's why I pay cash for everything."

Then knowing in my heart it was a mistake, I said, "Well, I could rent a car for you."

"Really? Are you sure? You are so amazing."

We went down together and rented Ben a Camry for a week. He paid me the sixty dollars a day in cash, so I felt fine about it.

I began to wonder if I could be that woman who visits her man "on the inside" on Sunday afternoons. Maybe I could. Ben would be so thrilled to see me. I would by far be the most attractive girl on visiting day. We'd both pick up the phone and touch each other's hands through the thick plate glass; I'd press my breast up against the glass like in the movie *Midnight Run*. Or maybe we'd meet at picnic tables and hold hands, since he did say it was white-collar crime, so it wouldn't be a maximum-security prison. I was beginning to think there was something kind of sexy about it. I totally understand how women fall in love with men behind bars. Think about it. The prisoners have all the time in the world to write long love letters to their women. This was something that Ben had already proven expert at. Unlike other men, they are not busy at work or traveling on weekends. They are never distracted while on the phone with their girlfriend because they are watching the fourth quarter of the basketball game. Instead, they are savoring every second, hanging on her every word as other inmates wait in line to call their baby mamas.

I had dated this cute actor guy, Reefer, whose live-in girlfriend left him for a Menendez brother. He had moved from Chicago to LA with his girlfriend, Anna, who didn't work, and every day when he came home from a long day of auditions, she'd be glued to the Menendez brothers' trial on Court TV. The brothers were on trial for brutally murdering their parents. Their defense was that their parents had abused them, while the prosecution argued that they murdered their parents for the money. The fact that they were living the life of luxury shortly after the murders helped prove it. One thing everyone agreed on was the brothers were hot. They were half Mexican and played tennis—it's a pretty sexy combination. One day when Reefer was home, he answered the phone and the computerized voice on the other end said, "Will you accept a call from the LA County Jail from Lyle Menendez?" Of course, he was shocked, especially when Anna came clean and said that she had contacted Lyle after watching him on trial every day wearing his collegiate sweater and tie. And, even better, they had fallen in love. She moved out, even after Reefer booked a sitcom. But in Anna's defense, Lyle Menendez's trial on Court TV did last significantly longer than Reefer's sitcom.

Anna ended up marrying Lyle. Their marriage was never consummated because his life sentence did not allow for conjugal visits. Years later, I watched a TV special on women who marry convicted murderers and Anna was featured. She said she came to visit Lyle one Sunday like she always had and saw him talking to another woman. She found out that he had been writing and talking to this woman on the phone. He had been cheating on Anna! She went on to say how disappointed all their friends were to hear that they were divorcing. I was thinking, Who are their friends? All of the couples who attended their wedding at the prison and shared a bite of the Twinkie from the vending machine? Did she host dinner parties with other couples and just put the phone on speaker with Lyle on the other end as they talked about the pot roast she made? What an asshole Lyle was to Anna. She left a cute working actor for him and this is how he repaid her?

But what women desire most from men is attention. And when men are in prison, they have plenty of time to give a woman attention. Only one hour a day outside of a cell left Lyle twenty-three hours to write love letters—apparently enough time to write to more than one woman. Of course, they are going to think you are beautiful. Who else are they comparing you to on a daily basis—the 250-pound female guard whose body is stuffed into the brown polyester uniform? But the women feel that they are the only thing their man has to live for, so they gain strength from that. Also on this same TV program, a woman said, "At least I gots me a man. Sure, he incarcerated, but at least that way he can't beat on me or have sex with other people. Well, at least not other women, that is."

Ah, how awful, I thought. But again, Ben is different, and we still didn't even know if he was going to actually have to go to jail, so in the meantime, I decided to just enjoy all the attention he was giving me.

After having the rental car for a few days, Ben asked me on the phone, "Did you read *Conversations with God?*"

"Yes, I did," I answered.

"And what did you think?" he asked.

"I thought it was interesting," I answered matter-of-factly.

"Interesting? You found it interesting?"

He was being very sarcastic. I didn't really know what to say. I wish I had said, "Yes, it's interesting that an author can create and write possible dialogue between himself and God, and people are buying it and preaching it like it was the Bible." But instead I just said, "Well, I haven't finished it, so let me do that."

On another day, I said I had to leave for a commercial audition and he said, "God, are you ever going to book one of those things?" That is something that you never say to an actor. He'd only known me for a couple of weeks. Imagine if he'd known me for the previous three years and actually seen how many auditions I went on and never even got a callback.

Ben was becoming less and less enamored with me and becoming more and more of a jerk. We were supposed to go to dinner after I went to the gym. As I finished getting all cute in the locker room, he called me to tell me that he couldn't go because—get this—he got in a car accident.

"In the rental car?" I screeched.

"Yes, in the rental car. What else do you think I was driving? Is that all you care about? Jesus, it's all about you, isn't it?" he barked.

"No, it's just I don't know what kind of insurance I have on it and what the deductible will be," I said.

"Well, don't worry. I will pay you every cent. I gave you the five hundred dollars, didn't I? Look, I have to go. I'll talk to you later." And he hung up.

The car still drove, but it had body damage. And, yes, he did give me five hundred dollars, but now he'd had the car for almost three weeks. So he owed me approximately another nine hundred dollars, and now this accident. I hadn't even seen him in the past four days. I started to feel panicked. Things had definitely changed. I knew now that his car was never stolen but rather repossessed. He wasn't pursuing me like before, and all I could think about was my credit card with that rental car on it that I didn't have possession of. I just wanted to get the car back so that I could return it and get back to what I and every other unemployed person plans to do when they're out of work: exercise, clean out drawers, reorganize closets, volunteer, and put photos into albums.

I attempted to get together with Ben on a couple more occasions, but he kept canceling or making excuses like, "I can't. I have to go to an AA meeting." Well, far be it for me to stand in the way of a former alcoholic and his sobriety, but I wanted that car back! If I mentioned the car or the nine hundred dollars he owed me, which was rising in sixty-dollar increments each day, he'd get all annoyed and offended that I was even bringing it up. This really stressed me out. I was unemployed, for Christ's sake! Long gone were the days of strolling the streets of Santa Monica slurping our Frappuccino and me overhearing him tell someone on the phone about this gorgeous, hilarious girl he'd met named Heather. And to think I even fantasized about buying a bunch of new sundresses so that I could surprise Ben in a different one each Sunday when I visited him in the prison yard.

I came to the conclusion then that is was over between Ben and me. I called him again and it went to voice mail. He must be seeing my digits and avoiding me, I thought. Just then, my phone rang. Oh thank God, it's Ben. I quickly thought to change gears. I feared the worst—that I would never get this car back. I don't know how I would explain that to my parents, the car rental place, or the police. "Well, you see, officer, I was unemployed and bored and looking for ways to procrastinate writing a script and thought it would be fun to hang out with a thirty-eight-year-old con man." Instead, I thought I would act casual, like I was still into him, and then once we were together, I would somehow snatch the keys, jump in the car, and escape back to the car rental place. Forget what he owed me. I just didn't want it to keep adding up or become a bigger problem than it already was.

"Hello," I answered, trying to sound as sweet as possible.

"Hey, Heather. It's Eric Fink." Oh my God—my old manager who tried to kiss me and still owed me $180. He was always easy to talk to and he was in AA, so I immediately told him about my current AA nightmare, Ben. Eric told me that AA people are the biggest manipulators there are. They've been through so much therapy and self-help; they only know how to use what they learned in AA to fuck over other people. I felt like saying, Oh, like how you convinced me that I was the next Rose-anne, only thinner and prettier, but all the while just wanted to have sex with me and not pay me back my $180? He went on to say, "And I know I still owe you that $160, and I'm going to pay you back."

Nice, I thought. You just trimmed twenty bucks off the grand total. But I didn't care. It was nothing compared to what Ben now owed me. I needed his advice on how to get this car back. He convinced me to call Ben on three-way calling. Eric would dial it from his phone so that Ben wouldn't recognize the number and would answer. Eric would just listen as I spoke.

So as Eric dialed him up and it rang, I said, "Are you there, Eric?"

"Yes, I'm here," he said.

"OK. Now don't say anything, and then I'll call you back after we hang up, OK?"

"OK," he said.

"Hello," said Ben, sounding like his old charming New York self.

"Hi Ben. It's Heather. Listen, obviously things have changed, and that's fine, but I need to return the car today," I said.

"Heather, I already told you the car is parked over by Icugini restaurant and I have meetings all day and I can't get to it," he said firmly.

"Fine, then I will come by and get the keys from you and get the car myself," I said.

"Wow! You are one passive/aggressive bitch," he said back to me.

Just then, Eric said, "Look, asshole. She wants the car back. It's over."

"Who the fuck is this?" Ben yelled.

"I'm a good friend of Heather's and she's pretty upset that you've been fucking her around, so be a man and give her the keys to the rental car," Eric replied.

"Fuck you both!" and with that, Ben hung up. Before I could talk to Eric, my other line started beeping. I clicked over. It was Ben.

"How dare you put some guy on the other line to threaten me? Do you know who you are dealing with? Do you know who you are fucking dealing with?" he screamed.

"Yes, I do know who I am dealing with and I want the rental car back," I said, raising my voice.

"It is over between us. You got that?" he yelled.

"Yes, I want it to be over. Can I get the car back?" I asked calmly.

He kept going on, saying how I was pathetic and how my dad really must have screwed me up and that I needed therapy and how I was never going to make it.

All the while I just kept persisting: "When can I come by to get the keys? What time?"

Finally, he said, "Fine. Come at six p.m., but you better fucking come alone. You got that?"

"Yes. See you at six."

As I hung up, I was visibly shaking as I dialed Eric back. I told him that I was going over at six. He wanted to come, but I hadn't seen him in years and he was still a douche bag who owed me money. I was grateful that he brought this mess to a head, but I didn't need another AA asshole to replace my current one. (Sorry, AA people. I know 99 percent of you are lovely, but I had just found the exceptions.)

I did, however, make plans to have another male friend, Pat, drive me to Ben's, since once I got the keys, he would have to drive me to the place where it was parked. I did not share the severity of the situation with Pat; otherwise, he would have insisted on coming up to the apartment with me, and I didn't want to exacerbate the hostage situation for the release of the keys to the rental car anymore.

I buzzed Ben from downstairs. "Hello," he said. "It's Heather," I said, and he buzzed me up. As I knocked on his door, I took a deep breath. He opened it and I took a step in as he shut the door behind me.

"The audacity you had to three-way call me. What the fuck is wrong with you?" he started in.

I calmly responded, "Can I please have the keys to the rental car?"

"You just want to throw what we had away over a stupid rental car?" he asked. Oh, like this romance had so much promise, you prick.

"Yes, I just want the keys and I'm gone," I said. Then Ben turned around with pure evil in his eyes, backed me into the corner between the front door and the wall, and began pounding his fists against the walls on either side of my head while screaming in my face: "Do you know who I am? I am a sociopath. Why are you such a passive/aggressive bitch?"

I shut my eyes. I didn't know what would happen next. He put his fists down, turned around, and walked away, saying,

"You know what your problem is, your problem is . . ." My eyes glanced down on the table beside me and saw the keys with the little Amir's car rental key chain. I grabbed it and ran out the front door as fast as I could to the elevator. I pressed the button and said, "Come on, come on," like I've seen in so many movies, such as *The Perfect Murder* when Gwyneth Paltrow realizes her husband Michael Douglas was the one who really wanted her dead, except the elevator did shut without Ben's hand stopping it, as he didn't bother to run after me.

When I sat down in the rental car I couldn't believe that at my age and with my life experience I found myself in this predicament. I could not tell my parents because ever since I was flashed twice in the same month at age nine and singlehandedly put one of the flashers behind bars, my family considered me something of a bad-ass.

I was walking home from school with my older sister Shannon, who was always running late for everything, I don't know why, mostly because she was always busy rubbing her eye, how she had any eyelashes left was beyond me—and on that day she was walking particularly slowly. There was an ABC Afterschool Special starting at 3:30 about a teenage girl who was pregnant with her soccer coach's baby and I wasn't about to miss a second of that, especially since it was based on a true story. So I walked way ahead of Shannon and a car drove up beside me and a man in his twenties asked me where Dumont Street was. At nine years old I knew every street, because I had delivered seven-pound pumpkins to every single house in the neighborhood, compliments of Bob and Pam of Country Club Realtors, for their annual Halloween pumpkin promotion. So I leaned in and proudly said, "Oh, you continue straight, then make a left on Kelvin, and you'll see it on your right." Just then he said, "What about this?" And out popped a big naked penis. I screamed, covered my eyes, and turned around as he drove off. I knew what a penis was. I had seen my brother's "appendages" though maybe only once or twice.

When I got home, I told my brothers and mom what had just happened. My brothers got out their auto magazines to show me pictures of cars for me to pick the pervert's car out, which I couldn't do. Then two detectives came to our house carrying a binder. I was afraid they were going to show me pictures of different penises to pick from. If I couldn't pick out the car I doubt I'd be able to pick out the penis. But they just asked me some questions like, "What was he wearing?" I said, "Overalls." I later realized this made no sense. *How did he get his penis out of his overalls?* As they were leaving they said to me, "If anything like this ever happens again, miss, the most important thing is to get the license plate number, even if it's just the first few numbers and letters." I felt like a failure for not being able to provide more clues; no way this crime was going to be solved in sixty minutes, or forty-four minutes with commercials.

About two weeks later, at recess, my friends and I were playing volleyball on the asphalt side court that was right next to the sidewalk and street. My friend Liz came running up to me in shock. "Look, that man over there is playing with himself." All the other little fourth graders were laughing, pointing, and covering their eyes, though a few were locked in a dead stare. Of course, this is a pedophile's dream. Nine- and ten-year-old girls in Catholic plaid jumpers, white kneesocks, and pigtails, jumping around playing volleyball—this pervert was a like a kid in a candy shop. I courageously walked over (as I had experience now dealing with the police) and indeed there was a man parked in his car sitting in the driver's seat with the passenger window rolled down. He was completely naked, no overalls in sight. He was not the man from two weeks before. I immediately told Liz to get me a paper and pencil. When she returned with it, I jotted down the license plate number and checked it twice. I felt so smart. I pretended I was Jaclyn Smith in *Charlie's Angels*.

I always insisted that I be Kelly, Jaclyn Smith's role, when my friends and I played *Charlie's Angels* because she had the best hair and the deepest voice. I mean really, is it any surprise that she can sell wigs, clothing, jewelry, bedding, furniture—how many collections can one '70s star have at Kmart? Whoever was the blondest got to be Farrah and whomever we liked least had to be Kate Jackson. If only I was wearing a white pantsuit, this moment would be complete. I flipped my locks back in an attempt to make them look feathered and walked straight to Sister Killion. "Sister, there is a man parked outside the fourth-grade volleyball courts, playing with himself," I stated like a prosecutor. "Glory be to God. Jesus, Mary, and Joseph! Girls, get away from the chain-link fence at once," she yelled. Once the flasher saw the long navy habit, visible handlebar mustache, and white nurse shoes running toward him, he lost his erection and drove off.

A few minutes later, all the fourth grade girl witnesses were in the office of our principal, Sister Patricia. Some of the girls were crying. I spoke up and proudly said, "Sister, here is the man's license plate number. The police will have no problem finding the predator with this. Case closed." We went back to class and within a half hour each of the girls who had seen the penis flashing got picked up by her mom and went home way early. I kept looking at the door and waiting for my mom. She never came. After riding my bike home, I walked into the kitchen and saw her sitting at the table drinking Maxwell House coffee and eating a bowl of dark cherries while studying her multiple listing sheets.

I said, "Mom, didn't the school call you and tell you what happened today?"

She looked up. "Oh yes, they called me at the office and said how you and some other girls were flashed." She acted like she got a call saying I'd forgotten my baloney and American cheese on Wonder bread.

"But Mom, did they tell you that I got the license plate number and that the police caught him within an hour and he confessed? It's an open-and-shut case, none of the girls have to point him out of a lineup or testify in court. Gosh darn it, we caught the dirty bastard!" I shouted as I slammed my fists on the table, like I'd seen in the last few minutes of an episode of *Cagney & Lacey*—of course I identified with the less dykey, thinner one.

"Yes, I know, Sister Patricia told me all of that." She said this as she brought her coffee cup up to her lips and dipped the tip of her tongue into it before taking a full sip.

"Well then why didn't you pick me up early from school like the other mothers did their daughters?" I questioned.

"Why, dear, you've already been flashed, I knew you were fine," she said as she bit down on the cherry while pulling its stem off. She swirled the cherry in her mouth and gave me a little wink as she spit her twenty-ninth pit into the napkin beside her.

I guess she was right, I was fine and stronger; however, it might have been a nice gesture after your daughter gets flashed for the second time in the same month to see that she not have to ride her bicycle home alone. As a nine-year-old I was convinced that I had singlehandedly sent this pedophile to the electric chair—wasn't that at least worth a scoop of Rocky Road ice cream at Baskin-Robbins? But in my mother's defense, she did have a two p.m. showing of a two-story Victorian.

Upon recollection of my double flashing experience, I notice that the damage on the car was significant, but what was more shocking was how disgustingly dirty the inside of the car was. There was trash everywhere, with old Jamba Juice and Starbucks cups reeking of mold. It said a lot about Ben that when it came to his home and his personal appearance, he kept it very clean and in shape, but when it was someone else's property, he had absolutely no respect. He was a total narcissist. I was so embarrassed to return it. I spent about fifteen minutes just throwing all the trash away. Then the Persian guy from the rental place came out to assess the car.

"This is not good! Big dent right there, and there, and there," he said in his heavy accent.

"Yes, I know. I also know I got insurance, so what is the deductible?" I asked.

The final damage was $2,146 and some change, which was all put back onto my credit card, minus the $500 Ben had paid me in cash, which, of course, was long gone.

When I got home, there was a message from Ben yelling the same stuff he had said before. I thought about going to the police, but for what? I really felt that if I just never contacted him, he'd go away, which he did. I clearly wasn't that important to him, damn. So naturally he never paid me the $1,646 he owed me, either.

A couple of months later, I heard through my parents' friends who lived in Ben's building that Ben was escorted out of his apartment by the sheriff's department. They talked to the owner of his condo and he hadn't paid any rent for the six months he lived there. Then I found out through another friend of a friend that shortly after his eviction, he threw a lovely party with his stripper girlfriend at his new home in the Hollywood Hills. How the hell did he get that? It was just like he was Michael Keaton in the thriller *Pacific Heights* with Melanie Griffith and Matthew Modine, where Keaton's character moves into their duplex by acting like he has a lot of money, but then once he moves in, he never pays rent and tries to drive them crazy as the worst tenant ever. At least, unlike Melanie Griffith's character, I didn't have to speak in a baby voice and Ben only destroyed a rental car, not my actual home.

This was one relationship I really had to thank my virginity for. Had I not been a virgin, I absolutely would have slept with sexy, manipulative Ben and probably become severely dick whipped. Who knows how long it would have gone on for or what lasting effects it could have had on me? I could have had his baby, gotten AIDS (remember, he did heroin), or worse, my FICO score could have dropped hundreds of points, and you know how important a good FICO score is. It wasn't like I was completely debt-free, but I wasn't routinely trashing cars.

I thought about writing a book called *Conversations with Ben,* where I would ask him questions like, "Did you ever have any real interest in me as a person?" And in my mind, he'd actually answer truthfully and say, "No, I was a criminal and you looked stupid. Who else is at Starbucks at ten-fifteen a.m.?"

 Bed, Keep It Tidy

After quitting Great Expectations and my terrible experience with Ben, I had still managed to put a couple of thousand dollars in the bank, and I thought, Now, should I save it or put it all toward paying off a credit card? What would my mother do? Gee . . . This was way too logical for me. I had what I considered ever more difficult choices to make: be a hypocrite and use it for the down payment on a new nose or join Sports Club LA, the Lexus of fitness. Sports Club LA was and is the most exclusive health club in LA.

I first heard about "the gym" when a friend of mine from college said, "Heather, if you want to find rich, powerful men in the entertainment business, then you have to join Sports Club LA." I thought to myself, How perfect—if I don't fall in love there, then perhaps I'll get an agent or an acting job out of it. Worst-case scenario: I'll actually begin exercising my outside obliques. I never really worked out, because I'm not good at exercise like that beefy yet small guy with a long blond ponytail who did infomercials as he grunted away pounds. As a child, I enjoyed Jane Fonda's workout tape, but only for her outfits, honestly. Leg warmers on my undeveloped calves were quite flattering. I just despised working out. I mean, the sweat? Gross! Mostly I was concerned that I had never really learned how to properly use the machines and was in constant fear that some trainer would come up to me and humiliate me by correcting my form in front of all the other audience, or, members. "Excuse me, Miss. That machine works your triceps, not your glutes. You need to come down from there before you become an insurance liability."

After receiving a tour of fitness nirvana, which included valet parking, a restaurant, spa, and Olympic-size pool on the top deck, where you could lay out and order drinks and food from cute waiters, I decided $1,300 up front and another $155 a month was a small price to pay to be part of this lifestyle. Anytime I went there, I dressed in a coordinated workout ensemble and was in full hair and makeup. It really wasn't a problem because I barely broke a sweat before moving from one machine to another. Some of the men I'd see there regularly had been fixtures on the club scene for years. One guy I always saw was in the process of getting hair plugs inserted. Each time I saw him lifting weights, he had a few more strands sprouting. I increased my reps with the number of plugs he had so that I kept building my stamina as his head of hair got fuller.

SCLA (as it was known) was also a great place to invite

people to my stand-up gigs. Many of the shows I did were "bringer shows," meaning that not only were you expected to bring people as audience members, but sometimes if you didn't get anyone to come to the show, the booker would not let you perform. Everyone I met at the chin-up leg-raise area or on the push-up mats was a potential audience member. The rowers were particularly sure bets because I stood facing them yelling all the details of the show while they would just nod. Approaching strangers and trying to convince them to come to a show must be what it is like to be part of a pyramid—or "a multilevel marketing business"—where everyone you meet from the hostess at IHOP to your mail carrier could be selling calling cards. "Could you use an extra ten thousand bucks a month? If you can't, then don't bother coming to the Radisson for a continental breakfast tomorrow." My line was pretty simple. I would approach my victims as they were running on the treadmill, working the cashier, or collecting trash on the freeway, and say: "Oh hey, I'm Heather. I perform stand-up every Friday night at the Belly Room in the Comedy Store, so come at eight o'clock, because I'm not just pretty, I'm pretty funny, and you get to hear my jokes about Catholic school and even LA traffic." Their general response was something like, "I love comedy. Let me know when you're performing next."

I would say, "This Friday night."

And they would say, "I can't this Friday, but call me and let me know the next time you're performing, because I will be there."

I would then say, "OK, but the next time is the following

Friday night at eight at the Comedy Store and the Friday after that . . ."

I eventually learned to just take their business cards (or in the case of court-ordered community service, their phone number at their group home) and add them to all the business cards that I had been collecting over the past couple of years in a glass fish bowl complete with pink sand and a bridge for the cards to swim through. When I was really desperate for people—like if I was doing a big showcase for a comedy festival—I'd just pick out the cards and start dialing. Oftentimes I had no recollection of who the people were or even how I met them. This tactic got me in trouble with guys, because they thought I was interested in them and wanted to get drinks afterward, and I'd be like, "Nope, this was it. Just the comedy and laughs. Hope you enjoyed. Thanks for coming tonight." It happened with girls, too. Some wanted to be friends and go shopping, and I'd be calling them back saying, "Oh gee, I can't, but do you want to see a Groundlings sketch show tonight instead?" It was still better than having my parents come, because during some of my more risqué bits, like how Caller ID is *69 and how coincidental that is when it's your ex-boyfriend calling, my mother would turn to the strangers seated around her who were laughing and say to them, "That's my daughter and what is so great is that she's still a virgin!"

The only results I was getting from SCLA, besides having fifty-year-old men approaching me at nightclubs, asking, "Don't you belong to Sports Club LA?" (at least they weren't asking me, "Didn't I choose you at Great Expectations?") was that each month I was $155 poorer, with only one-sixth of a pack of abs. No matter how much I tried to get famous director Michael Bay's attention while squatting repeatedly, he failed to look in my direction. I got angry with myself that I didn't "seize the day" and show up dressed like a 1940s nurse when he was casting *Pearl Harbor* and start jogging on the treadmill in my white nursing shoes and pin curls, and maybe start a conversation with Michael about my love for the jitterbug, Rosie the Riveter, and my war efforts, including how I wore a yellow ribbon for three days during Desert Storm.

However, I did make one girlfriend, Lily, who was in the fashion industry and only dated very rich older men. She was a self-proclaimed gold digger but also proud that she wasn't like some of the girls at the gym who really were prostitutes who were paid in cold hard cash as opposed to just having your rent paid. Lily really wanted to get married someday, too, and hoped that the fifty-eight-year-old, thrice-divorced, ears, nose, and throat doctor would be her knight in shining sinuses. All my friends at the time were in serious relationships, so it was great to meet someone who also enjoyed fine food at someone else's expense and parties that always seemed to include security, a guest list, catered hot hors d'oeuvres, and a sushi station.

Lily was thirty-three years old, but swore me to secrecy. She didn't want her fifty-eight-year-old boyfriend to know how old she really was because that could kill the deal. I told her that one day he would find out, like my dad did when my mom lied and said she was twenty-three when she was actually twenty-four. As the priest searched for her baptismal certificate when they were making plans to marry, she finally came clean. Lily had told him that she was twenty-six, like I was. Ageism is a serious thing in Hollywood, especially when the annual Playboy mansion Halloween party invite list is involved. Lily got both of us on the list. I dressed as Xena the Warrior princess (a cheesy, campy, syndicated show about a hot girl who swung a sword around in medieval times and her very lesbian-acting sidekick). I had the costume and wig from a sketch I did at The Groundlings. Lily wore trashy lingerie, along with 90 percent of the other female partygoers, and got the Little Bo Peep outfit complete with the corset and platform thigh-high leather boots. Halloween has always been every girl's excuse to dress like a slut and every ugly guy's chance to hide behind a mask. One Halloween, I danced with Zorro all night, begging him to remove his mask. When he finally did, he had one eye going in a completely different direction before making a right, a left, then another right.

When I attended my first Playboy mansion party, they took my photo and phone number. I guess I looked cute enough, because they invited me back to several parties. The problem was I couldn't just bring a cute girlfriend with me. I had to send in her head shot plus a full-body photo and hope she'd be approved. Forget even considering bringing a guy. The parties were 85 percent women, 11 percent men Hugh Hefner's age, and 4 percent attractive guys under forty. Talk about slim pickings. The most exciting thing that happened was when I narrowly avoided tripping over Verne Troyer by the Grotto. Thank God, the food was delicious, because that soon became my main priority for attending these things. After downing a few drinks, I found myself at the buffet piling on their signature lamb chops. I was a little leery about where to sit, since so many of the girls wore only painted lingerie. I didn't exactly want to plop down where one of them had just been dining, not for fear of their paint rubbing off on me, but more the fact that vaginal discharge happens to the best of us. Just because you have a G-string spray painted on, doesn't mean you're really wearing one, no matter how amazing the artwork is. But most Playboy parties end the same way at around 2:40 a.m.: this is when everyone left suddenly decides at the same exact moment that it's time to get the fuck out of there and go home. The problem is you have to take these little shuttles from the mansion back to a parking lot at UCLA where your car is parked. There are only a few shuttles running so people would panic in fear of being stranded at the Playboy mansion and pile into the first shuttle they saw, knock people over, sit on top of each other, it was total mayhem. It was as if that shuttle bus was a lifeboat aboard the *Titanic*.

Lily invited me to other great parties with celebrities and industry types. At one of these shindigs, I met Kato Kaelin, the most famous houseboy and key witness in the O.J. Simpson trial. My brother-in-law knew him from when he used to work at car shows, so that was my way of introducing myself. He was probably so happy that someone actually knew him from something other than from living rent-free at age thirty-five and hearing three thumps the night of a double murder. I made out with Kato at some mansion near the porta-potties, but there was really nothing there. It had been a few years since the trial and his star was fading faster than his looks. Somehow the shoulder-length shag with blond highlights is less acceptable at forty than at thirty-five. What can I say? Life is not always fair. However, he was kind of funny and proceeded to call me and invite me to other great Hollywood parties.

At one of these parties, I was thrilled when a William Morris talent agent approached me. He was about thirty and a typical agent, a little on the short side, well dressed, with dark rimmed glasses and full of charisma. It turned out he represented Tom Arnold, so I immediately went on about myself and my comedy aspirations, including the fact that I had just performed a one-woman show featuring many Groundlings' characters as well as personal stories. It seemed at the time that anyone breathing had a one-person show, but he seemed impressed. He gave me his card and told me to call him on Monday to set up an appointment and bring the tape of the performance for him to watch.

That Monday morning, I made my coffee and began to peruse my latest batch of business cards collected over a busy fun-filled weekend. Among them were a few sales girls and gay guys who worked in retail from the Beverly Center shopping mall. I had added to my credit card debt buying a new outfit, but I justified it because they said they'd come to a show. Suddenly the William Morris agent's card popped up. I stared at its raised printing and heavy card stock. I hated calling agents, but I wasn't getting any younger, and I thought, Heather, seize the day. You need to make this happen. Have some balls and call. I took a deep breath, a bite of my Thomas's English muffin with its natural crevices trapping just the right amount of butter, and dialed. Then I hung up, remembering that agents were very busy in the morning when the breakdowns (what was being cast) came in, and I should call after noon. Good—a reason to procrastinate for another three hours and go to SCLA to trove through the members. At 12:10 p.m., I called.

"William Morris Agency. How may I direct your call?" said the perky receptionist.

"Alan Weinstein's office, please," I said politely.

A moment passed. "Alan Weinstein's office. How may I help you?"

"Yes, may I speak to Alan?" I asked.

"Who may I say is calling?" she questioned.

"Ah, this is Heather McDonald," I said as silence set in.

"From what company?" she pressed.

Oh shit. I wasn't from a company. Should I tell the assistant I met him at a party? "We're friends," I blurted out. I figured if he didn't remember, then nothing was going to happen, anyway.

"One moment please," she said.

A few minutes passed when I heard, "Heather, how are you?" It was Alan.

"I didn't know if you'd remember me from the party Saturday night," I said cheerfully.

"Of course, I do. Are you going to come by and see me today?"

Wow! All the other times I set up agency appointments, they were set for weeks ahead or they told me to just keep inviting them to any shows I had, to which they rarely showed up—except for the time after courting a small talent agency for two months, I finally got all eight agents to come see me at a cool stand-up place called Luna Park. When I attempted to put them on the list, the asshole running the room wouldn't do it, so I had to put another sixty-four dollars on my credit card. My set went great, and so did the guy's after me. They passed on me and signed him.

So to have a William Morris agent—the crème de la crème of Hollywood agencies—want to see me that very afternoon, I was beyond ecstatic. We made plans for me to come in at four p.m. That was great because it gave me just shy of four hours to get ready, and I spent every moment doing just that. After many wardrobe changes, I decided on a black short-sleeved bodysuit, which snapped at the crotch like a leotard, it was like a onesie for an adult, a short pleated black miniskirt, and black mules. I felt although it was tight and skimpy, being all black classed the look up a bit. My hair looked good, but it would look especially good if I kept my sunglasses on top of my head, giving my hair false height without appearing like I was trying too hard.

I walked into the lobby, gave my name, and was directed to the elevators. A hand stopped my elevator door from closing, and attached to it was Shari Belafonte, the famous daughter of Harry and a beautiful actress in her own right. Now I was sharing an elevator with Hollywood royalty. At my floor, I was met by a girl about my age who was a bit nerdy and a little frump-a-dump. No offense Tri Delts, but she would have been one of you if we were still at USC. She eyed me up and down and said, "I'm Amanda, Alan's assistant. Follow me." As I followed, we passed a large conference room with priceless views of the city and spastic assistants with headphones speed walking through the halls. She turned her head back to me and asked suspiciously, "So how do you know Alan?"

"Oh, we met at a party over the weekend," I answered.

"What a surprise," she said sarcastically. What the hell was that supposed to mean? I wondered. "I'm a stand-up and perform at The Groundlings and just wrote/starred/directed and produced my own one-woman show to a one-night-only sold-out performance." Although I bragged, I failed to mention that the theater only held ninety-nine seats and every single attendee knew me personally. I continued, "Alan is dying to see it! He asked me to bring the tape so he could view it when he has a chance."

"Great. Have a seat. I'll tell him you're here," she said in a rather snippety tone.

As I sat on the black leather couch, she got on her computer but kept looking back at me. When I'd catch her scoping me out, she'd give a polite smile and resume typing. What is with this bitch? Has she never seen a potential client before, or maybe she was thrown by how cute a female comic can be?

Just then, Alan came out to greet me. "Hi Heather. Come on in." As I stood up to follow him, I realized I should have worn flats. He was even shorter than I remembered. "Have a seat," he said as he extended his hand toward a love seat up against the wall. I thought it was a bit strange that he didn't offer me the seat across from his desk but figured it made sense when he sat right next to me. We talked about frivolous things as I kept trying to wedge in information about my burgeoning comedy career, dropping subtle hints about how much money he could make off of me when I have my own sitcom cleverly titled *It's Heather*. Suddenly, Alan put his hand on my knee and looked me in the eyes, which he could do since we were both sitting down, and said, "You know, I noticed you right away when I saw you by the lion statue at the party."

"Which one?" I laughed. The home was owned by a prominent LA Persian businessman. Persians are known for their love and overuse of feline statues, columns, and an inherit need to build a balcony off of every bedroom in their architectural endeavors. I was feeling a little uncomfortable and wanted to keep the conversation on track, so I reached into my purse and pulled out the VHS tape of my show.

"So here is my one-woman show. I really appreciate you looking at it," I said as I held it in my hand.

Alan then leaned over and began kissing me. Something came over me and I began kissing him back, getting pretty into it. He was sexy for an industry Jew. His lips were soft, his skin was well moisturized, and he smelled of expensive cologne. If my nostrils weren't deceiving me, I'd say it was Emporio Armani Diamonds for men. Something was so sinister about making out with an agent that it was reminiscent of the old days of the casting couch back at a time when not all casting directors were either women or gay men. Things were getting steamy and I was definitely aroused. He felt my breast over my body suit and I didn't stop him. I don't know what I was thinking, just that there was something really exciting about this whole sleazy experience. His hand then went up my thigh to where the front of my bodysuit and the back of my bodysuit met with three small snaps. As he attempted to unsnap those suckers, I pulled his hand away. I was not about to be fingered by a William Morris agent through a Donna Karan bodysuit. Represented, yes. Fingered through Donna, no.

"Alan, what are we doing?" I asked. "I'm starting to wonder if you're really interested in my body of comedic work or just interested in my body," I said. I thought that was a pretty clever line.

"No, no, I am, but I'm also interested in you," he said as he leaned in closer so that I could feel his hard-on on my thigh.

I left my head shot and tape, and Alan assured me that he was going to watch it. As I walked out of his office, the assistant gave me a disdainful look and I felt pretty disgusting. As I got in my car, I talked to myself out loud as I often do. "Heather, what the hell? That is not you. What were you thinking?"

A couple of nights later, my phone rang at one a.m. It was Alan, drunk and wanting to get together right then. He was begging to come over, and when I said no, he kept giving me his address for me to come over. "Have you watched my one-woman show yet?" I demanded.

"No, but I really want to. I've just been really busy." Then he started getting really dirty and graphic in an attempt to have phone sex with me. He even brought up the freakin' bodysuit and how sexy it was under my schoolgirl skirt. My skirt was just pleated; it wasn't plaid. This guy was a sick fuck. I hung up and could barely sleep. I was so mad at myself for getting in this situation yet again. How could I be so stupid? I'm from LA—well, sort of, the Valley. I graduated from college. I didn't just fall off the turnip truck. The next morning, I grabbed the bodysuit and threw it in the trash can, the nonrecyclable one, because I didn't want that thing making a comeback in any way, shape, or form. Then I promptly called William Morris and got Alan's assistant on the phone to inform her that I would be there in an hour to pick up my one-woman show VHS tape. She started to question me, but I stopped her and firmly said, "Just have it waiting. I don't need to see Alan. I want my tape back."

I was so sick of this shit. I had recently dumped an ineffectual talent manager who had become a caterer, but for a year I didn't have the strength to break up with her. Finally, I went to her apartment—oh yeah, she ran her catering/managing business from her apartment, too—to pick up my remaining head shots, résumés, and Groundlings sketch tapes that I had paid for and given her to send out. To my surprise, not one of the tapes or head shots was missing. In over a year of managing me and making her own salad dressings, she hadn't sent one out? Yet I was so codependent I felt guilty that she hadn't made any commission on me. As soon as I got my tape in my hands, I bolted out of William Morris. I was so upset that I decided to work out my anger at Sports Club LA.

While working out, I was actually perspiring on my forehead for the first time. A little while later, I saw Lily. She was all excited to see me because the fifty-eight-year-old boyfriend was having a dinner party and she wanted me to come. Of course, I wanted to come. A free gourmet meal? Are ya kidding?

The dinner party was for ten people and Lily's boyfriend was quite delightful to talk to. He was really funny and liked to drink. They sat me next to some record producer that the fifty-eight-year-old had known since they were kids growing up in the Bronx, I'm assuming, sometime during the Great Depression. I barely spoke to the record producer guy all night. He was tall but completely gray with a set of brand-new porcelain veneers. The next day, Lily called me and said that Richard was really interested in me. "Who the hell is Richard?" I asked.

"He's the music mogul," Lily replied excitedly. "He's produced records for everyone. He wants the four of us to go out."

"Lily, no. He is not attractive, and no offense, but he's really too old for me," I said.

"Heather, he's a multimillionaire and normally only dates twenty-year-old models. The fact that he's interested in you means he really likes your personality," she said encouragingly.

"Fuck you, Lily," I laughed.

"No, I just mean you're pretty, but . . ." I cut her off.

"Lily, I just can't. I can't imagine getting together with him." She went on and on with his résumé, where his mansion was located, how he could have any woman in LA, and how I should be so thrilled. She finally convinced me to go to some black-tie charity event with the three of them. Since I never went to events like this, I was curious, and any opportunity to dress up, I so loved. We sat at Clive Davis's table, who I was told was big in the music industry, but I had no idea who he was until *American Idol* came on some years later and realized that I was at a pretty spectacular event with Clive Davis, the man who signed Kelly Clarkson and discovered Whitney Houston. If Lily had done any research besides financial on these people, I could have leaned over and told Clive how much I loved *The Bodyguard*. Richard, like his fifty-eight-year-old best friend, was smart and fun and charming, but I just could not force the attraction angle.

What if I really was a gold digger and learned to fuck really well so that he was pussy whipped and I got him to marry me? Then, like the rest of the Beverly Hills gold-digging wives, I would get bored and wait for him to simply die. But, I mean, let's face it—old people are just not dying like they used to. You see this type of woman all over Beverly Hills. She's about sixty, with her shiny face, due to one too many dermabrasion treatments, pulled back so far that she can barely see through her catlike eyes as she pushes her ninety-year-old husband in his wheelchair, cursing the day Viagra was FDA approved. This was clearly not her plan when she was thirty and married her sixty-year-old billionaire groom. Her plan was that after ten years he'd die and she'd only be forty and still hot, but things don't always work out as planned, especially when part of marital duties include counting pills and emptying colostomy bags.

After the charity event, Richard called me a few times, but I did not return the calls. I wasn't in the music industry, so I couldn't even talk myself into going out with him one more time for the sake of connections or networking. Some time passed and Lily's fifty-eight-year-old refused to let her move in, so she decided to put her foot down and only fuck him on the weekends, because it was summer and he had rented a beach house in the Malibu colony for three months.

So on a Thursday night, Lily picked me up for a night on the town. We decided to begin with drinks at the Four Seasons

Hotel in Beverly Hills. At the time, their bar was pretty happening with rich, successful guys. At the bar we had a few drinks bought for us and were talking to a small group of businessmen when I noticed Jerry Seinfeld walk in and sit at a small table with another writer-looking guy. Now, Lily was in the fashion industry and not entertainment. Even though when I first introduced her to Bill Maher, she didn't know who he was, after fucking him, she attested to his huge penis, however she did know who Jerry Seinfeld was. I gritted my teeth like a ventriloquist auditioning on *America's Got Talent* and said to Lily, "Jerry Seinfeld is right there. Don't look to your left." She managed to look nonchalantly. This was during the eight or ninth season of Seinfeld. He was single and I always felt that I was kind of a Catholic Shoshanna Lonstein. Shoshanna was the big-busted girl he had dated for six years, but they had broken up. I kept thinking to myself, Seize the day. Take advantage of this situation. Just say something. Do it, goddamnit.

"Lily, I'm going to say something to Jerry Seinfeld."

"You are?" she questioned. For someone who clearly didn't make the best decisions, even she was apprehensive about this move.

"I need to take control of my life, and luck is where opportunity meets preparation. Here is my opportunity. He's in front of me and I'm prepared to say hi. Besides, I don't get much cuter than this," I said with confidence. However, there is no place in that luck-meets-preparation aphorism that mentions what happens to luck when you throw three Cosmopolitans into the mix. But there was nothing stopping me now. I opened my

Lancôme powder, checked my lipstick, and walked right over to Jerry's table and said, "Hi, Jerry. I'm sorry to bother you, but I'm Heather McDonald and I'm a comedian, too."

Jerry looked at me, smiled, and very nicely said, "Hi Heather. This is my friend Bernie."

"Hi Bernie," I said, and then I felt so welcomed that I pulled a chair over from another cocktail table, and plopped down. "I just love the show," I said enthusiastically. Their table for two was up against a wall, so naturally I sat at the side that was open in between them.

"So what do you talk about in your act?" Jerry asked.

Well, now that just opened the floodgates. I talked on and on and on about The Groundlings. I explained that I talked a lot about dating. Suddenly, I had an out-of-body experience, much like those who die for a few minutes and watch themselves from on high while being revived by paramedics. That's what happened to me. I saw myself literally dying and I couldn't stop the tragedy. I started getting really physical, doing bits from my act, laughing at my own jokes, grabbing my own breasts to make a hilarious point when we were interrupted by the cocktail waitress.

"Can I get you something to drink?" she asked. Jerry and Bernie's drinks were full, so I said, "I'll have an Amstel Light, thanks." Then I turned to Jerry and Bernie and said, "No worries. I'm not going to stay here all night. The second I get my beer, I'll leave."

I continued with what I thought was entertaining when Lily came over to the table. I introduced her and then she said to me,

"We have to leave soon. My friend Amir said he could get us in to SkyBar, but we have to meet him there by eleven." What an idiot she was! Who cares about Amir and the SkyBar? Hello—I'm talking to Jerry Seinfeld here; there could be a guest spot in my future. "OK, I'll be right there," I said to Lily. "Don't mind her, anyway. What was I talking about? Oh, that's right, me, anyway . . ." Just then, the cocktail waitress returned with my beer and left, but I simply continued. "So I'm supposed to be showcasing for the HBO Aspen Comedy Festival this year, but . . ."

At that point, Jerry interrupted me and said, "Heather, I thought you said when you got your beer you were going to take it and leave." I just about died.

"Oh, of course. I'm so sorry," I said. "It's just that we need to discuss some business here."

Jerry said disgruntled, "Let me pay for this."

As I dug into my purse, I could only find two dollar bills with M.A.C. lipstick smeared all over them. "Wait—let me pay for my beer," I insisted as I frantically searched for a five- or ten-dollar bill.

"You don't have to. Really, it's fine," Jerry said. Of course, it's fine. He's making over a million dollars an episode, but I continued to insist on paying for myself.

"No, no. Well, here you go. Good luck on your ninth season, like America isn't tired of that," I said laughing, getting in my one last attempt at a joke. Having no other cash on me, I left the two crumpled lipstick-stained dollars on the table and joined Lily at the bar.

"We have to get out of here now," I said, pulling her off the bar stool.

Driving over to the SkyBar, I was still reeling from the experience. At first, I thought Jerry was a little rude. Then I realized how obnoxious I was.

I learned a valuable lesson. For example, carpe diem, seize the day, does not mean accosting someone important while they're trying to enjoy some tiger shrimp at a restaurant.

"I knew it was bad when I saw your hands flying everywhere while you were telling a story. That's why I went over there to try to save you and get you to leave," Lily said.

"Well, thanks for the attempt. It's the thought that counts." This wasn't the first time Lily had saved me. I went through a brief stage where I wore a hairpiece I bought at a kiosk in the mall to give me that height I love at the back of the head without having to tease my hair. I adored this hairpiece until the night I was talking to a cute guy at a house party and I leaned up against a gothic-style wall sconce and when I went to follow him to the bar I realized I was attached to it. My hairpiece had gotten stuck on it and was lifted off my head and hanging there in the hallway. So I quickly went back up against the wall and fit my head back under my Bump-it-type hairstyle for a good hour, until I was able to summon Lily to get me loose. She was thrilled it happened because she was annoyed I was wearing, with my naturally thick hair, what she described as a "dead squirrel" on my head in the first place.

"Hopefully, SkyBar will be fun. Something needs to save this night," I said, exasperated.

SkyBar was at the Mondrian Hotel on Sunset Boulevard and was the total hot spot. It was outdoors around the hotel's pool, and there were big white beds for hanging out and sipping cocktails. About an hour into the party, I noticed Vince Vaughn. The hit movie *Swingers,* which starred Vince, had come out about six months earlier. He was there with one of the other cast members from the movie who was not as famous. They were right by us, so I ended up talking to the less famous guy, who was very friendly.

Even though I was wildly attracted to Vince from the moment I saw *Swingers*—from his height, to his face, to his fantastically fun personality—after the Jerry Seinfeld *Poseidon Adventure,* there was no way I was going to even look in Vince's direction. Besides, girls were coming up to him from all directions. Then, somehow, he started talking to me! For the first time in my life, when someone I was attracted to talked to me, I didn't flirt back. He asked me if I was an actress. I told him my deal, but this time nonchalantly mentioned The Groundlings, figuring he'd probably never even heard of it. But he was completely intrigued and asked a million questions. Each time another model-looking girl came up and interrupted us, he was polite and then immediately came right back and talked to me.

I had never dated an attractive, successful actor. I figured I really didn't have a chance, but Vince kept coming around all night, even when we began to leave. He stopped Lily and me and said, "Well, where are you guys going now?"

"We're going home. It's two," I said.

"Well, I want to see you perform at The Groundlings," Vince said anxiously.

Finally, someone was impressed by The Groundlings, the same theater group that the William Morris agent/mauler and Jerry Seinfeld couldn't give a shit about.

"OK. I'm in the Sunday show, so it's every Sunday," I said rather unexcitedly. I'd been through this before.

"I'll be there this Sunday. What time?" he asked.

"It's at seven p.m.," I said cautiously. We exchanged numbers and I told Vince to call me on Sunday if he was coming. I told a few friends about how cute and nice he was in person, along with the horrific Seinfeld story. It made for a pretty eventful evening. I didn't tell anyone about Vince wanting to come to the show, because I thought there was no chance.

Around four p.m. Sunday, I checked my messages after rehearsal. There was a message from Vince saying that he wanted to come and to call him with the details. I called back, got his voice mail, and said that I'd leave two comp tickets for him at the box office. I still didn't tell any of the other cast members, because I figured he wouldn't show up. After the first few sketches were performed, I went out to the box office and asked if my comps had come. The answer was no. Fine, who cares, I thought. Now I don't have to be nervous.

Then in our group dressing room as I checked my makeup, one of the other members of Groundlings who was not performing that night said, "Hey, that guy from *Swingers* is here."

"What? Are you sure?" I asked in a bit of a panic. It was my turn to go out and act out my improvisation. I admit I was thrown and did not do my best at turning the audience's suggestions into a hilarious scene. After my performance, Vince was there with a childhood friend who was visiting from Chicago. It turned out he didn't use the comps that were offered and insisted on paying. What a class act! He was really complimentary to me and to everyone else in the cast. Admittedly, I felt like the hottest girl in Hollywood in front of my Groundlings friends for having a funny, babeish movie star there to see me. I turned to Vince and said, "Well, thanks so much for coming."

I was sure that was it, but then he said, "Well, are you going out with the rest of the cast for drinks? Do you mind if we come along?"

"Oh, of course. We're going to the Snake Pit, down the street." This place fit the name perfectly. It was a total dive perfect for snakes. Vince bought everyone drinks. Then he said he wanted to go somewhere else with just me and his friend, so, of course, I was up for it. It was funny because he drove a similar car to the one he had in *Swingers.* It was some big classic boat, which seemed to float through the back road on our way to Los Feliz, where the hipper bars, all of which were featured in *Swingers,* were located.

Vince was hilarious; he was incredibly quick on his feet and had me rolling with his obscure references and philosophies on life. The night finally ended at four a.m. in the parking lot next to The Groundling's theater to retrieve my car. It was a little awkward, because the childhood friend was with us the entire night, including when Vince dropped me off. I kissed him anyway, with the embarrassed friend squatting in the backseat. Vince was a great kisser and he said he'd call me. I didn't expect him to.

The next day, I told my friend Josh, a fellow stand-up comic the whole story and he said, "You know, tonight we're showing short films, and one of them is *Swing Blade*. It's a parody putting the Billy Bob Thornton character into the set of *Swingers*." He added, "It's hilarious. Trust me, you should tell Vince to come."

I debated for a few hours and then I thought, Oh well. At this point, what do I have to lose? I left him a message, saying, "Hey Vince, its Heather. I'm going to Largo tonight, and I'm sure you've already seen it, but they are showing *Swing Blade,* so just thought I'd let you know. Bye." I felt that was very low-key. I didn't expect him to show up, so when I chose my outfit, I opted for a casual button-down shirt and navy miniskirt, an outfit that would have been appropriate to wear to a real estate showing in Encino. I didn't even shave my legs. Though the hair wasn't quite braiding length, but my legs weren't the smooth silkiness I would have if I ever thought another human might be touching them.

At the club, I sat with Josh and watched the acts. I watched the door for Vince. No Vince. See, I told myself, he's not coming. The *Swing Blade* movie started to play, and halfway through the six-minute film, Vince walked in with the same friend. I stood up and brought them over to our table. I felt pretty cool having Vince Vaughn at my table. Comics who knew me but had never spoken to me before, because my comedy wasn't perceived as "alternative" enough, kept coming over. They'd say hi to me, then immediately introduce themselves to Vince and compliment his work as an actor and then never look in my direction again during the conversation. I couldn't help but wonder what a life like that must be like. What would it be like for a woman who is with someone of celebrity-level importance? Sometimes you can see it when the male star is being interviewed on the red carpet and then finally Joan Rivers turns to the wife and asks, "And who are you wear— . . . Oh, I'm getting word we're going back to you, Melissa."

We hit a couple of more bars that night. Besides Vince's childhood friend, some comic who knew Vince from kickboxing had invited himself and wasn't really flirting with me but more challenging and pestering me at every turn. I asked Vince what this guy's deal was and he said, "I think he's like the kid in elementary school who pulls your pigtails because he really likes you." Vince asked me what my dream job was and I said to star in my own sitcom. At the final bar, The Horse and Carriage—a total dive, a place where 90 percent of the patrons have never even heard the word *loofah,* let alone ever used it, but apparently cool to the hipsters in Hollywood—our bar stools faced each other and he suddenly grabbed for my three-day stubbly calves. I kept moving his hands so that he wouldn't feel the patches of leg forest.

Thank God we were interrupted by yet another girl coming up to Vince who had taken acting classes with him. She looked at me politely and said hi, then got about an inch from Vince's face in an attempt to have an intense conversation with him about the Meiser method. It was about emotions and some repetition exercise where two actors would look at each other and say, "I'm smiling," and then the other actor would say, "You're smiling," and then back, "Yes, I'm smiling," and so on. This could go on forever, so I was hoping they'd start doing it, because that way I'd have an opportunity to escape. I told Vince and acting-class ho that I was going to the bathroom. I started heading toward the back. When I saw that he could no longer see me, I ran out of the bar and started sprinting to the corner. I pressed the crosswalk button on Sunset about a hundred times, as if that ever helps, and ran to the Rite Aid across the street.

In a total panic, I screamed at the cashier, "Where are the Bic razors?"

The cashier was a black woman, who looked at me and said, "Ma'am, I am helping another customer right now. If you need help, you need to find another store associate."

"That's OK. I'll find it myself." I didn't want to piss "the associate" off and felt that based on basic demographics, she'd most likely never even heard of the movie *Swingers,* let alone seen it or understood the importance of me having smooth legs immediately. I ran through the store like a crazy woman, first going down the shampoo isle. Why isn't it with the other toiletries? I thought. Come on, come on. Then I was in the toilet paper aisle, which only had paper goods. What the fuck? Finally, I found the little travel-size Bics. I grabbed a pack and some shaving cream and looked for the bathroom. Wait, I thought. That's a crime. I need to buy them first. I started running down the aisle to the black lady with an attitude. There were three people ahead of me. I had already been gone for at least five minutes. I immediately added up the time zone and calculated, If I'm gone any longer, Vince is going to think that I left for good and go home with acting-class ho.

So there I was at the Rite Aid, holding my bag of disposable razors and shaving cream. The line was moving like midnight zombies. OK, I'll buy it, I thought, and I'll run back and then shave them in the bathroom at the bar. With each nanosecond that passed, I was more and more conflicted. I even considered shoplifting for a moment and calculated I'd be in prison until at least four p.m. the next day, and I had a Fiber One cereal commercial callback at noon. Just then, another checkout opened and I cut in front of an old lady, threw a ten at the cashier, told him to keep the change, and ran. I prayed to the Lord Jesus and tried to explain that I doubted the old lady had a hot movie star to get back to and I'm sure she didn't care that I cut. When I got a few steps away from the front door of the bar, I slowed down, put the razors and cream in my purse, and walked in calmly. Just as I stepped in, I bumped right into Vince.

"Where were you?" he asked.

"I just went across the street to get some gum," I lied.

"Oh, can I have a piece?" he asked.

"I just realized I left the bag at the checkout. I'm so stupid," I said.

"Well, the bar is closing, so we have to go," he said as he put his hand on my back to lead me out. I looked back longingly at the restroom, desperate to put my leg on the sink and break in that razor with my fur.

The four of us, Vince, childhood friend, annoying comic,

and me, got into Vince's car and drove the annoying comic to his apartment. When I stepped out to let the comic pass, he said, "We'll have to go out again, when he's not around." That was just bizarre; being with Vince was even making other guys like me more. Then Vince drove to my car and parked behind it. The childhood friend was once again sitting in the back. He was really becoming a third wheel.

"So what do you want to do?" Vince asked.

What I wanted to do was have a good dry-humping old-fashioned blue-balling session with Vince Vaughn. So I said, "Well, we can go back to your place and hang out." I figured I'd go to his bathroom immediately upon arrival and shave these legs and then our make-out session would get started.

"Well, there's some other friends of mine staying there, too. We could go back to your place," he suggested.

All I could think about was how disgustingly messy my room was, not to the point of being on an episode of A&E's *Hoarders,* but it was pretty bad. Let's just say it looked as if Amy Winehouse and Courtney Love were roommates. Besides an unmade bed, there were my dirty G-strings and wigs from Groundlings' sketches strung everywhere. My first thought was that we could make out in the living room and he'd never even see my messy bedroom. But the friend was going to have to come with us, so he'd have to hang out in the living room with us, too, which would have been beyond awkward. I said, "It's really late and I think I better leave." I kissed him again with the friend sitting in the back. Being a virgin, Vince would have been just another notch on my chastity belt, but even if I wasn't and

Vince was going to have me every which way including Sunday, there was no way I was going to bring him to that disaster of a bedroom. It was simply too shameful.

Vince said he was going out of town but would call me the following weekend to get together. Well, that weekend was Memorial Day weekend, which was when *Jurassic Park 2* came out, and he was in it. I never heard from him. Instead, I called him a few times and left messages like, "Hey, I'm trying to see your movie, but it's not playing anywhere. Ha, ha." Needless to say, my calls were never returned.

Luck is where opportunity meets preparation, so if you want to get lucky, my advice is to always shave your legs, pick up all worn G-strings from your bedroom floor, keep it short when meeting with the most successful sitcom star of all time, and never wear a bodysuit around a William Morris agent. In fact, just never wear a bodysuit, especially if you ever plan on getting "lucky"!

Ray

Getting tired of LA guys, my friend Sarah and I decided to go to New York for four fun-filled exciting nights. We didn't have much money, so we were going to stay with one girl-friend for two nights and then split up. She'd stay at a different friend of hers and I would stay at our newly married girlfriend Nicole's apartment for the remaining two nights. I had been a bridesmaid in Nicole's wedding, which was incredible. I remember the two gay male wedding planners whispered in my ear at the rehearsal dinner that the wedding cost upward of four hundred thousand dollars due to the exclusive location, exorbitant number of flowers, and special effects lighting. It would have been a perfect evening if it wasn't for my date, Jeff.

Jeff was a game show producer for a trivia show and just a few years older than me. (I was twenty-seven.) Everything was going great, we'd been on a few dates, and my dry humping skills were up to full par. He'd call when he said he would, so I thought he'd be the perfect one to invite to the "Black Tie strictly enforced" wedding. Besides, Nicole's father was a TV director, so I knew Jeff would be impressed, as Les Moonves (the president of CBS) would be in attendance. However, like so many of my unconsummated relationships, after a few weeks, Jeff started acting a little dickish. At dinner one night, he bragged about how when he took me out, he told his boss I was a different publicist each time so that he could put it on his expense account. Even if he did that, why would he tell me unless he was trying to hurt me? It's every girl's self-esteem booster to know she's some man's corporate write-off.

For the rehearsal dinner, in which all of the bridesmaids were invited with a date, feeling this relationship was on the brink but it was too late to invite someone new, I called Jeff and said, "Hey Jeff. Don't feel like you need to attend the rehearsal dinner on Thursday night, too. You can just come to the wedding on Saturday."

"No, no. I want to come to the rehearsal dinner. I'll be there. The Four Seasons at seven p.m., right?" he asked. Since I had to be at both events early, he was going to meet me at the rehearsal as well as the wedding. I was excited for all the festivities. Being one of Nicole's bridesmaids had become a part-time job between the numerous showers, fittings, and mandatory meetings on necessary undergarments, length of pearls—12-inch, not 14—and hairstyle, all to be worn down and professionally blown straight. Only the bride would wear her hair up. I was looking forward to all my hard work coming to fruition. I tried to remain positive and told myself that maybe I was misreading Jeff and that we actually had a chance of making it.

At the cocktail reception at the rehearsal dinner, Jeff came up to Tara and me, and the first thing he said was "Wow, Tara! You look amazing. That is some dress." Tara, who was a bridesmaid, too, did look great, but to say that first to her without even a hello to me? I tried not to make a big deal out of it. Throughout the dinner, he continued to hit on Tara anytime her boyfriend was not in earshot, at which she just laughed as I took another gulp of Chardonnay. At the end of the night, as we were waiting for our cars, Jeff didn't make any attempt to get me to go to his place or even kiss me, even after I hinted with "So what do you want to do now?" His response was "Go home, and you should do the same. You look tired." I knew this relationship was going nowhere fast and I still had to spend the entire epic eight-hour wedding with him.

All that night I couldn't sleep. It reminded me of the brazen rude behavior of my first Mary Duque Deb ball date, Eric Kellog. I didn't put up with it then, so why put up with it ten years later? The next morning, I called Tara to discuss the night and said, "Tara, he was so hitting on you right in front of me. He gave you three compliments throughout the night and not one to me. I think it will really bum me out to have him at the wedding when I know for a fact he could give two shits about me. I'm going to call the wedding planners and say he has influenza so they can rearrange the seating."

"No, Heather. You are going to regret not having a date there. All eleven bridesmaids are bringing either their husband or boyfriend. Even the fourteen-year-old junior bridesmaid, Nicole's cousin, is bringing some guy she is seeing from her AP algebra class. You can't be a dateless bridesmaid at twenty-seven."

"Tara, now you sound like my mom when I just wanted to go stag and dance with my dad all night at the Valley Deb ball, but she was horrified. Who gives a shit? I know half the people there. I'll have plenty of people to talk to," I said. Tara went on to defend Jeff, saying that she thought he was just trying to be funny with her and still really liked me, finally convincing me to stick to the plan to meet him at the Pacific Palisades mansion at four p.m. for the ceremony.

Since I was the tallest bridesmaid, I was the first to walk down the aisle and stand over on the left-hand side. I looked out to smile at Jeff and make the best of this day only to find him fixated and smiling ear to ear while staring at Tara as she slowly walked down the aisle to the song they always use in Hidden Valley Ranch salad dressing commercials, standing on the right-hand side of the altar. He never even looked on my side for the entire wedding ceremony. Afterward, he found me at the bar getting my first of many glasses of Veuve Clicquot champagne. Again, right in front of me, he complimented Tara on her dress. Hey asshole! I'm wearing the exact same cream off-the-shoulder Vera Wang dress as she is and we're the same size. Then the videographer came over to interview me. I did a funny, then sentimental toast, and when it was over, Jeff said, "Do you always have to be on?"

"No, but I am going to be *on* when a camera is on for something that is going to be around forever." When we arrived at the tent for the reception and I had a few more champagnes in me, as much of a jerk as Jeff was, I still wanted a date to talk to, dance with, and make out with. But every time I leaned over to Jeff or tried to get him to dance to "We Are Family" or "The Macarena," he refused. So I danced with the four-year-old flower girl, the fifty-year-old divorcées, even the grandpa with Alzheimer's who thought he was, in fact, dancing with the bride. When none of them were available, I danced by myself. Halfway through the night, I thought to myself, This is what it must have been like to be Princess Di when she was married to Prince Charles, always trying to get his attention at fancy state dinners and him just turning her away trying to spot Camilla. At the end of the night, Jeff drove me back to my apartment and kept the motor running as I gathered up my bouquet, program, and heels, and then I turned to him and said, "Look, let's just be honest. You're clearly not into me anymore, so I'm never going to hear from you or you see me again, so . . ."

Then he said, "Heather, you're drunk. We'll talk in the morning. Just get out of the car." So I did. And the next day, Jeff left me a message, saying, "Heather, in spite of what you thought, I had a really good time at the wedding and I want to see what your plans are this week so we can get together, so call me back." I have to say it felt very satisfying to delete the message and never talk to him again.

It was fun shopping and hanging out with Nicole in New York. She and her husband's place was tiny, as most New York apartments are. She had to keep all the fine china she'd gotten from her wedding tucked under her bed. She set me up on her sofa with a pillow and blanket, but for someone my height, it was pretty uncomfortable, because it was a loveseat. I was still grateful, as there was no way I could afford a hotel. On the flight back with Sarah, who was Nicole's premarriage roommate in LA, I said how my neck and back were hurting so much. Sarah asked, "Why?"

I said, "Well, I slept on Nicole's loveseat and for me at five-feet-nine, to crouch up in a fetal position for two nights in a row can't be good for my spinal cord."

Sarah looked at me in shock and said, "Nicole didn't pull it out for you?"

"What do mean pull it out? What out?" I questioned.

"That couch pulls out into a double-size bed."

I couldn't believe it. Nicole had a coffee table in front of the couch filled with meticulously arranged crystal Tiffany candlesticks that people had given her as wedding gifts, so the only explanation was that she didn't want to bother moving them in order to pull out the couch and give her poor bridesmaid a decent night's sleep after she flew six hours in coach on a red-eye to see her. What a horrible hostess. She must have thought I'd never find out that the loveseat pulled out into a bed. To have been able to stretch and lay flat on my stomach all night would have been magical. I never had the balls to confront her until now, so if you're reading this, Nicole, next time, move the goddamn candlesticks, bitch.

A couple of nights after returning from New York, I was at a nightclub in Santa Monica and ran into some guys I knew from college. I was chatting with them when the one standing to my right said, "Heather, you don't recognize me? It's Ray Smith."

Ray Smith was a Sigma Chi, and his mother and my mother were in the San Fernando Valley Gamma Phi Beta alumni group and had planned many functions and parties together. In fact, that is how I met Ray when I was nineteen. He was transferring from Cal State University Northridge to USC, and my mom took me to a party at their house and introduced me. I thought he was really nice and cute but shy. In college, he joined Sigma Chi and took me to one party. As we were making out pretty hard core on the roof of his fraternity house, he kept saying, "Heather, I can't do anything with you. My mom knows you." I just know that my mom told his mom that I was a virgin and his mother probably warned the shit out of him not to do anything with me. Thanks, Mom. Way to watch my hymen. I mean, I barely got a grind out of him. So after that party, we'd see each other on campus and say hi, but that was about it. Now I was twenty-seven and he was thirty. We talked all night at the club. He wanted to walk down to the beach, but I wasn't about to do anything with him without a proper date first.

The next day, he called. I remember I was on the 3rd Street Promenade and my phone was dead, so I went to a pay phone to check my messages. I was so excited that I called him right back from the pay phone. Ray's father was in the film industry and he had worked with his dad for many years. Now he was on his own with his own small production company and studio to film commercials and music videos. I was impressed. We went out to dinner that night and he told me how he had a serious girlfriend for many years right out of college, then her best friend revealed that she'd been cheating, and then the best friend became his girlfriend for the next three years. They had just broken up a few months ago. Both of the exes were Pi Phis, so I immediately looked them up in my Greek Legend yearbook at home. The first girlfriend was a pretty half Latina girl and the second was a total blonde, blue-eyed beach girl. Well, Ray certainly didn't have a type, except maybe cute.

I had a fresh unopened package of birth-control pills and decided to start taking them that following Sunday. My gynecologist had given them to me for free after he brought in his medical assistant, Maria, who was twenty-six, the second oldest virgin he knew, so that we could meet, which was awkward, as I laid there in the stirrups and tried to make small talk with her. He wasn't pushing the pills on me, but even he at sixty years old felt it was about time I got that cherry popped.

This wasn't the first time I had taken the birth control pill. I had begun it three times before—once when I was with Phil the hand model, then again when I was dating Santa Barbara, then the last time, when I was seeing Divorce Dad Dan the Marching Band. I knew I had to take it for a month for it to be most effective and in each case the relationship ended before the month's pills were consumed, so I repeatedly found myself in a virgin state with a half-empty prescription.

When I was in high school, my mom was fifty and was still getting her period. This concerned me because I knew she wasn't on any kind of birth control yet she and my dad were still having sex. This was confirmed each time I tried to open their door in the morning to ask for a check for school and then to my total disappointment found it locked! What was my irresponsible premenopausal mother thinking? I knew my mother did not grasp the rhythm method and that is how my sister and I came to be. My dad used to joke, "Your mother can't count a calendar." I was becoming more and more concerned that my mother was acting recklessly with her vagina, and at her age, if she were to get pregnant, there was a very good chance there could be complications, plus she worked full-time. I kept pleading with her, "Mom, this is serious. If you have a baby, I'm not taking care of it. I've got two honors classes next fall, this is my year." She would just laugh and try to blow me off. Until one day in the car she couldn't take my badgering anymore and she pulled over and said, "Listen, I'm going to tell you something but you cannot tell your brothers or sisters. After you were born your father had a vasectomy. He struggled with the decision, being that it is against the teachings of the Catholic Church, but his friend introduced him to a priest in San Juan Capistrano who blessed it, so it's OK." What a relief. Had they just been honest with their daughter from the beginning I wouldn't have lost so much sleep over it.

Over the next few weeks, Ray and I saw each other a few times a week. He lived in a nice apartment building just off Sunset Boulevard. I'd go over there after I performed someplace close by and I would sleep over after an evening of everything else, but . . . One time I was leaving another one of Lily's old rich men dinner parties and I called him. He was at home writing a screenplay. I was driving on the freeway from Encino back over the hill to Santa Monica, where I lived, and I asked, "So do you want me to come over or not?" He could not make a decision. He kept hemming and hawing. I finally said, "Ray I'm at that point on the 101 where I either cut into the 405 on my way home or keep going straight to Hollywood—make a choice." This part of the freeway always has traffic, so I always cut in at the last minute and wave to the person behind, pretending like I just got into town and had no idea that this freeway entrance came so quickly. Also at a certain time in the morning, right where the 101 and the 405 meet, it lends itself to incredible lighting, perfect for tweezing your eyebrows as you scooch along at two miles per hour.

"Come on, Ray. What's it gonna be?" I asked.

"Yes, come over," he said. I immediately crossed four lanes, barely escaping a potential pile-up.

That night, as we were once again on his bed wearing just underwear and making out passionately, I said, "OK. Come on, let's do it."

"Really? Are you sure?" he asked.

"Yes, but use a condom." So that was it. I was buzzed, of course, from the drinks I had before, but it was fine, not mind-blowing by any means. I was just trying to do my best to appear as though I had done this monumental act before. There was no way I was going to tell him before or afterward that this was my first time. I stuck to that plan.

The next morning, we lay in bed and talked just like we had the other mornings when we hadn't had sex. I kissed him goodbye at my car. When I got home, I picked up my phone and called my two sisters and two best friends, Tara and Liz. I started each phone call exactly the same by saying, "Hi, it's Heather! Well, you've been waiting for this call for twenty-seven years. Congratulations to me, I finally did it, I'm officially no longer a virgin." Besides the four of them, no one close to me knew I was still a virgin.

That night, Ray met me at the Laugh Factory to watch my stand-up set. He had never seen me before and it was just OK, not the worst but certainly not my best. He was really sweet and supportive and took me out for drinks and dinner at Red Rock afterward. He said, "About last night, did you have a good time?"

"Yes, of course, I did," I said reassuringly.

"Like a really good time or just a good time?"

I knew what he was getting at. Did I have an orgasm? Well no, I didn't, but I wasn't going to let him know that, so I said, "Yes, I had a really good time." I followed up the statement with a Sarah Palin wink. I went back to his place that night and did it a couple of times, faked an orgasm like so many women had long before me, and I started feeling like a real adult for once.

Ray was good about calling and keeping plans. When I came over to his place after I filmed a small role, he took me to Spago's to celebrate. The following morning, as we talked in his bed, I turned to him with all the confidence in the world and I asked, "Ray, what am I to you?" He looked up at the ceiling and said, "Heather." I was positive he was going to say, "Heather, of course, you are my girlfriend." Instead he said, "Heather, I don't want a girlfriend right now. I just got out of two three-year relationships and I really need to focus on my career." I swallowed and quickly went to every acting skill I had ever learned and said, "Oh, me, too. I don't want a boyfriend right now, either. I was just making sure so we were on the same page."

As I drove home that morning, I was sad but OK with everything. I liked Ray a lot, but I wasn't in love with him. I decided to really back off because I knew this wasn't going anywhere. He called me a few times and I called him back, but we never made plans and I never saw him again. Once it was out there—"Heather, I don't want a girlfriend"—I just didn't want to be that booty call and try to push a relationship. I was grateful. I lost it to a nice, fun, cute, and most important, normal guy who never knew he was my first. So he didn't receive an unwarranted compliment of being "the one" and he also didn't feel forced into having a relationship with me because he was my first when he really wasn't into it. That would have just wasted my time and possibly in the end really hurt me.

I still had my morals and my values but also my birth-control pills, which I continued to take religiously. If I did meet another nice normal guy I was attracted to, I had the tools and knew how to in fact "do it."

So this was officially an end of an era—an era of blue balling to my heart's content. And though I was forced to relinquish my crown as Queen of the Blue Balls due to a technicality (no longer a virgin), I still love the art of blue balling and practice it to this day.

9 LA, LA, Just Addicted to Crack

I met Matt one Thursday night during the summer between my freshman and sophomore years of college at a bar just minutes from my parents' house. Matt was twenty-five which really seemed much older than me at the time. He owned a three-bedroom, one-and-three-quarters bath, 1,100-square-foot contemporary ranch house in Reseda and seemed very successful. Most drug dealers are.

I ended the relationship once I suspected that he was doing more than remodeling houses. But eight years later, he introduced me to Peter, for which I will be forever grateful.

I didn't see Matt again until several years later when I was working as a writer on Keenan Ivory Wayan's late-night talk show. My first day on the job, I walked up to the catering truck to get lunch and there he was. It was Matt's catering company. Wow! He had gone from supposedly building houses to building sandwiches. Matt still had his big white teeth, straight nose, and he wore a blue and white bandana wrapped like a surfer dude around his head to cover the receding hairline, which had been evident eight years earlier. At this point, I assumed there wasn't much left to run your fingers through. I suppose the look worked in a Brett Michaels kind of way, minus the eyeliner and eyelash extensions.

"Matt," I said in amazement. "Gosh, it's me, Heather McDonald."

He was shocked, to say the least, that I was a writer. In my humble opinion, this struck him as being kind of annoying. Hello! Didn't he remember how witty I was when he took me to the Elton John concert and upon returning from the bathroom I announced, "The bitch is back"?

As I complimented him on his culinary ingenuity to use not one but two kinds of cheeses in a quesadilla, we quickly became friends again. It wasn't even in the playing field that we would be anything more than that. Matt was no longer moonlighting as a marijuana sales rep, but he was still a loyal customer of the weed. He also did quite well catering for the studios.

We would talk on the phone—he in his catering truck, me still in my 1992 red Toyota Celica—about all of our dating nightmares and triumphs. One day he simply said, "I think I have a guy for you!"

My first question since I was in diapers has always been, "How tall?" Not only am I tall, but I'm also a fan of big hair and platform stilletos.

Matt said that my potential new guy was six-three.

"Really?" I replied. "How old?"

"I think he's, like, thirty-three." Matt continued chopping cucumbers.

"That's good, since I'm twenty-eight. Kids?"

"No," he said.

"Ever been married?" I asked, going over my "Heather Husband Must Haves" list that I readily had at my disposal.

"No," Matt said. Then he hesitated a little, "Ah, but he was engaged."

Now to me, this was as intriguing as a two-hour *48 Hour Mystery* on CBS. It meant that at one point, my potential date had asked a woman to marry him! Marriage was on his radar. "What happened to the fiancée?" I continued, hoping that, unlike a *48 Hour Mystery,* she did not go missing after a day of sailing with him.

"She broke up with him," Matt replied. By now, it sounded like he was scraping the cubes into a bowl.

"Perfect," I told myself. "Not only is she still breathing, but she dumped him." This wasn't the typical potential bride stands at the altar; groom doesn't show; jilted bride sues, is featured in *New York Magazine,* gets her groove back, sells the film rights to her story, and Kate Hudson is set to star in the major motion picture. He wasn't the one who freaked out and dumped her and may one day regret it. She had simply moved on.

"What's his hair doing?" I said, nearing the end of what could be called badgering the witness. I didn't want to hurt Matt's feelings, since he was losing his hair—and many bald men are extremely attractive—but I'm a gal who loves a full head of hair to which I can apply a variety of Paul Mitchell products. Traditionally, I've also always been attracted only to dark-haired men who are not Persian. Matt assured me that Peter had all of his hair so this was all sounding very positive.

"Where does he live?" I prayed it was not in the City of Industry or any other town where major water parks are advertised.

"Sherman Oaks, in a condo." Sherman Oaks is very nice and only about a ten- to fifteen-minute drive from the Westside, totally respectable.

"Own or rent?" I asked, wondering why Matt wasn't irritated by such interrogation.

"He bought it a couple of years ago."

Yeah, a homeowner, and now there is equity in it, too! Yes, we can live in it for a while, then sell it and use the profit to buy a two-bedroom cottage in Malibu Canyon, eventually working our way to a property on the water!

Matt had the green light to go ahead and set up the date. This conversation took place in October 1998, but Matt was such a flake that he let things lapse. I guess he got a little preoccupied with cleaning out a bong and failed to make the introduction.

Then in December of that year, Matt said, oh so casually, as he plopped a huge helping of macaroni and cheese onto my plate at the studio, "Oh yeah. I remember there was something I was supposed to tell you. I talked to Peter."

"Who's Peter?" I asked. At this point, I was seeing Chris,

an extremely cute former USC football player who wasn't doing much with his life but looking cute. This was totally good enough for me. It was nothing serious, but every time I would accept that it had been a week since I had heard from him and convinced myself that I would never hear from him again, he called. And each time, I told myself, "I am making out with a USC running back! Sure, he was on the team six years ago, but still!"

Matt went on to explain that Peter asked him, "What's up with that Heather girl?" Peter, too, was annoyed that Matt hadn't made this rendezvous happen yet. I told Matt just to give Peter my number, but Matt never managed to do that, either . . . because potheads are about as reliable as, well, potheads.

Then one Saturday in January, Cute Chris called me. At this point, it had been almost two weeks since I had heard from him.

I kind of felt bad for Chris. He played in the Rose Bowl in his twenties, and now in his thirties, he was no longer catching passes but rather delivering muffin gift baskets to overweight realtors as part of his job as an assistant to an escrow officer. He was even back living at his parents' house in Topanga Canyon. I did not find out about his two "housemates" until a few dates in. I was mortified and chose to keep that tidbit to myself when describing him to my friends. Instead, I said, "What's great about Chris is he's really close to his parents. He even manages to talk to his mom every day." I wasn't really lying. I just left out the part where the talking took place when his mother was tucking him into bed.

Chris told me that our mutual friend Jamie was having a birthday party at the Mexican restaurant El Cholo in Santa Monica at eight that evening and asked if I'd like to go with him.

I immediately thought about Matt. He and Peter were friends with Jamie, too. (Oh my God! Oh my God! I was already feeling tingles of excitement!) Would they be heading there, too?

Just in case, I told Chris that I would meet him there.

As soon as I hung up with Chris, I called Matt and asked him if he was going. He said yes and then I asked (so nonchalantly, as if it were an afterthought), "Oh, is that Peter guy going, too?"

Matt replied that indeed he was.

I told Matt that I was going, too. I'd be "technically" on a date, but "officially" I wasn't that into him anymore, so I was going to drive my own car just in case the Peter guy and I hit it off.

Matt replied, "Yeah, whatever, so I'll see you there."

It's amazing that this was truly a blind date, which in this era of technology really doesn't exist anymore. Today, if you can't find a photo of the person your friend is setting you up with on the Internet, your best bet is to stay home on a Saturday night and watch *America's Most Wanted*. All I could think about as I waxed my upper lip to prepare for my plural dates was that Peter was thirty-three, tall, with a full head of dark brown hair that I could style and pet while watching episodes of *The Real World*. When I walked into the bar area of El Cholo, I said my "heys" to the people I knew. No sooner did I give a quick kiss to Cute Chris, when I felt a tap on my shoulder. I turned around and this guy with the biggest smile ever said, "Hi, I'm Peter."

It was a moment frozen in time, like Nicole Kidman's pale white forehead in *Cold Mountain* etched in my memory forever. Peter and I talked that whole night while he bought me piña coladas with the conveniently placed little umbrellas just in case it rained in the bar. I never even glanced in Chris's direction the entire night.

As the crowd started to disperse, Chris, while walking toward the door, called out, "Bye, Heather."

"Bye," I replied with a casual wave. I never saw or heard from Chris again. When we were dating, though, he did tell me that the last three girls he had been with met their husbands immediately after going out with him. I couldn't help but be hopeful.

The crowd from El Cholo was moving to another bar called Renee's. Peter asked if he could drive me there. Well, of course, I said um, yes. He had a new black Ford Expedition—again totally respectable—not a Ferrari but not a Mini Cooper, either. He was cool and nice, and yep, I really liked this guy.

At the bar I was surprised how aggressive he became when he leaned in and I asked, "Are you seriously trying to kiss me right now?"

He replied simply, "Yes." I loved that. There was nothing I hated more than when a guy would ask, "Can I kiss you?" This is especially gross on the must-see TV series *The Bachelor*. What are you going to say? "No?" I mean, I think it's all a little pussi-fied. Guys just need to go for it, not to the extent of date rape, but to the point of a man taking control.

Peter took me back to my car and followed me back to the apartment I shared with my Buddhist/Catholic/agoraphobic roommate, Debbie. Because of her, there was no way I was going to let him see her sitting in her footie pajamas, eating Ben & Jerry's Cherry Garcia ice cream, and watching *My Cousin Vinny* for the thirtieth time.

I made out with Peter to the point where I was getting pushed into a large flower bed outside of our building in which the back of my black micro-miniskirt was being poked by the prickly rose thorns. I love dry humping, especially on a first date.

As Peter saw me to the front door, he said, "I will absolutely call you tomorrow."

I was on high alert. You know, that level where orange turns into red on Homeland Security's radar.

The next day, I waited and waited, and he didn't call. I checked my home line several times, making sure it was plugged in. I checked my cell phone battery and continued to call both my voice mails throughout the day just to make sure that I didn't miss his message, even though I had never left my apartment.

What the fuck? I thought. Maybe he's just waiting trying to be cool. But at this point in my professional dating career, noth-ing surprised me.

The next day, Monday, Peter finally phoned. He asked me if I'd like to go out next Wednesday night or Friday night.

I chose Friday because I wanted to have a date on the weekend. That was the only reason. That and the fact that even if I sat at home Saturday night, at least I could tell my friends that yes, I did have a date that weekend. Ever since I was a little girl and sleepovers became popular, I hated the feeling I would get on a Friday morning when I didn't bring an overnight bag with me to school. This was a reminder that no one had asked me to come to their house.

I have always hated not having plans, whether it depends on being with another fifth-grade girlfriend or a thirty-three-year-old man. Even today, I have to have something to look forward to, whether it's a stand-up gig, a dinner party, or even the unveiling of a new free tasting item at Costco. I like plans.

Also, by choosing Friday, it left more days in between seeing each other, which that book *The Rules* had driven home. The dating bible book also taught me to always appear like you're busy and have other suitors, so having Cute Chris at our first meeting had probably helped things. Most guys are naturally competitive. It gave Peter something to work toward, a goal to get me to pay attention to him instead of Chris.

Friday night came and I buzzed Peter in. When I opened the door, he was even more handsome than I remembered. He drove us to Chaya Venice, a very hip California cuisine bar and restaurant. As we waited in the bar, he said, "I feel like having a martini."

"I feel like a martini, too," I said. "Wow, we have so much in common. We both like strong vodka drinks and olives." When we sat down to order, I asked, "Do you like to share?"

He said, "Yes."

"Oh my God! Oh my God! I like to share, too. This is all just simply crazy." Then I asked, "What are the chances that two people like to drink martinis and share appetizers on a first date?"

As we were enjoying the many other little dishes that we ordered, Peter asked me, "Do you like to fly first class? I like to fly first class."

Of course. I mean, who doesn't like to fly first class? Like someone is ever going to say, "Actually, I prefer to be wedged in between two 300-pound strangers with a seat that doesn't recline and to be centimeters from a volcano-size pimple on the passenger's neck beside me that I fear will explode onto my four-dollar energy bar with every passing sneeze." From that night on, I knew he was the one. He was my first-class guy!

The day after my first date with Peter, I had been invited to a couple's baby shower in Hollywood Hills. Unlike a lot of women, I actually love baby showers and bridal showers. I love the feeling I get around four in the afternoon buzzed off Chardonnay and full from cake and Chinese chicken salad. This being a couple's baby shower was even better because there were all these cute guys there.

My friend's husband was in chiropractic school. So these guys were hot and could crack backs. Quite a combo! I am addicted, much like someone addicted to crack, to cracking my back. I first learned to self-crack back in eighth grade listening to Duran Duran's "Save a Prayer." I would come home from school, turn it on, and then stretch and twist until I got as many audible cracks and pops as possible.

Recently, I was watching A&E's *Intervention,* a documentary-style TV show where they show real addicts sniffing cocaine or shooting up heroin and then their family does an intervention by reading letters to the addict about how much their addiction has affected them all. I always have to watch until the very end of the episode. That's when they play the happy music and write on the screen that Susie completed ninety days of rehab in South Carolina. I wipe my tears and feel so relieved until another paragraph pops up stating that Susie relapsed six days upon returning home and has gone back to sniffing computer keyboard cleaners.

Halfway through an episode about a woman addicted to Vicodin, I realized that I was addicted to crack backing! Or is back cracking? Who cares? I know what I mean.

Several times a day, this woman would go to random pharmacies and pay strangers who had prescriptions for their Vicodin. She couldn't function or think about anything else until she got her fix. I realized that I was the same way.

When I ask someone to crack my back—which most people can do if I stretch out facedown on the floor and they press on my spine—it is torture until the person actually does it exactly right. As I lie there waiting and begging for the crack, it's all I can think about. When I hear a good strong pop, it's so euphoric I practically orgasm.

In a way, I'm just like heroin addicts wrapping a rubber band around their arm, waiting for the hit. I look for the same hit with a crack in my back. I'll even ask a stranger to do it. If I find someone at work willing to crack me, I'll lie on the filthy carpet and back-crack. I don't care. They don't even have to be a licensed chiropractor or even someone I like. Lay me flat and twist one leg to the opposite side, cross my arms, squeeze, and turn my head so that it's facing the other direction. Just crack my back if you ever meet me. I'll love you forever!

The first time that I was professionally "cracked" or "adjusted" was by this huge black chiropractor. He pushed on my back once and it was like someone took a piece of bubble packing wrap and twisted it and it popped—that delicious sound that only bubble pops can make. I'll be honest: I've been chasing the dragon ever since, and it's never as good as the first time. But until Promises in surf-pounding Malibu opens up a wing for backcrackaholics, I guess I'll just have to live with my addiction.

Maybe one day if I become famous enough, I'll have my own Heather McDonald Center, just like Betty Ford. The center will bring the insatiable need to hear one's spinal cord snap, crackle, and pop like a bowl of Rice Krispies drenched in 2 percent milk to the forefront of the medical community. We'll have big black-tie charity events to raise money for the wing, showing videos of recovered back crackers throughout the hundred-dollar-a-plate dinner.

I don't know if my self-awareness of my back-cracking addiction made me not want to flirt with these cute chiropractic students, like an alcoholic turning down a bartending job because the temptation to indulge would be too great, or if I chose not to flirt with the hot chiropractors because I already met the man I was destined to marry.

When I told my friend Tara about my date with Peter and my lack of interest in the chiropractors, she immediately said, "I think this could be the one."

"Don't jinx it!" I screamed.

My friends and I used to believe in jinxing things. It's the direct opposite of *The Secret,* a book, a movie, a way of life, a Hallmark card, detailing how the secret to success lies in envisioning what you want in minute detail and asking the universe to hand it over. For example, if you want, say, an infinity pool, just make a vision board depicting exactly what you desire. Cut pictures of your dream house and pool from *Architectural Digest* and glue snapshots of you and your loved ones splashing around in the water; park that red Porsche off to the side and say out loud: "Universe, I want an infinity pool." You can add pictures of anything or anybody you might want, too. (Mine would include a photo of really good abs!) Then you're supposed to hang the board above your bed or across the room, where it's the first thing you see when you wake up and the last thing you see at night, and one day it will all come true!

I do question this philosophy a bit. If this vision board thing really worked, wouldn't every teenage boy be banging *Sports Illustrated* bikini models?

But at the time—in those pre-*Secret* days—we thought if you said it out loud, then you'd jinx things and keep them from coming true.

Regardless of the jinxing, I knew in my heart, yes, I think Peter could be "The One," but so as not to jinx it, I kept that to myself. Peter and I dated very consistently, seeing each other every weekend and once or twice during the week.

Then about three weeks in, Greg, a good-looking guy I knew through friends, asked if I'd like to go to the Bachelor Ball with him. A Bachelor Ball is a charity event for bachelors to bring dates. Everyone dresses up as famous couples. It was basically all former USC fraternity guys. Peter had not asked me out for that Friday night, so according to *The Rules,* I was to accept this other invitation, especially because at this point, Peter and I were not exclusive. That Friday night as I was driving from my parents' house to my apartment in Brentwood to get ready for the Bachelor Ball, my cell phone rang. It was Peter.

"So what are we doing tonight? Do you want to see a movie or go to dinner and rent a movie?"

This was all so great! This couldn't have worked out better. I needed to write those two New York bitches who wrote *The Rules* a proper thank-you note because I followed Peter's question with line 23 from *The Rules,* Chapter Five: "Always appear to have other male suitors even if you do not and have not been on a date in a decade."

"Oh, I can't. I have plans tonight," I said, savoring the pause that I knew was the result of Peter feeling insecure. "I have this charity event to go to." I knew that he would find out about it through our mutual friend, Jamie. "So, I'll talk to you tomorrow," I said and hung up.

As I continued driving, I immediately sat up straight,

opened up my sunroof, and tossed my head about in sheer delight. That's right, dude. I have other plans. I am a creature like no other. Sit and ponder that all night, Peter.

The Bachelor Ball was fun. Greg was entertaining and attractive enough, but as we made out in my apartment afterward, I couldn't help but feel like I was cheating on Peter. I just wanted Greg to leave. I guess he picked up on my telepathy, because he did.

The next morning at about seven forty-five, my phone rang, waking me up. It was Peter asking if I wanted to meet him for breakfast in Beverly Hills. He was absolutely checking up on me to see if (a) I was there and (b) if someone else was there with me.

Obviously, he was relieved when I answered and agreed to meet him. We ended up spending the whole day together. After breakfast, we went Rollerblading in Venice Beach.

By the way, does anyone but me even Rollerblade anymore? I don't even think it is very good exercise because all you're doing is rolling. I usually hate active dates, but Peter was a good Rollerblader and helped me down a steep hill. The last time I went Rollerblading with a guy, he made fun of me for rolling too slowly and rolled ahead of me the entire date. What a freaking dick—and not a very big one from what I remember of his spandex shorts.

By our eleventh date, Peter had been blue balled pretty badly. I had spent the night numerous times after long make-out sessions where we were both completely naked, and every time I'd say, "No, I don't know you well enough," Peter would just say, "OK," and we would both go to sleep, until a couple hours later when I'd feel someone knocking on my back door and it was Peter with a big boner. Then we'd make out some more, in which I'd turn him down again, and the knocking would restart around seven a.m. That is the best. I do miss the knocking. The only knocking I get now in the middle of the night is from my kids wanting to come in my room.

I had lost my virginity a couple months prior to meeting Peter with Ray, but we had only done it a few times. So when I finally decided in the middle of a Mel Gibson movie I was watching with Peter that tonight he was going to get some, I started laughing, which brought me a lot of attention, since the movie was not a comedy. Again, I just love being a woman. The woman decides when and if you are going to have sex. I decided yes, I want to make love to Peter, and we are going to have full-blown intercourse in about an hour and nine minutes from now, and sweet Peter is just sitting next to me completely confused as to why I can't stop laughing.

Like I had always promised myself, I was taking the birth-control pill regularly for the past six months, so when the moment came and I said, "OK, do you have a condom?" Peter was so shocked, he asked, "Are you sure?" And I was sure. It was very good and fun and I was madly in love.

10 The Courtship of Mackenzie's Father

Months passed and we were all set to spend the Fourth of July weekend with Peter's brother Tim, a divorced daddy from Las Vegas. Tim, Peter, and I went to our friend's party in Manhattan Beach. This was my first time meeting Tim, and I obviously wanted to impress him. In retrospect, Tim is an easygoing guy who's worked in casinos his whole life. It wasn't like I was meeting Jackie Kennedy Onassis at Le Cirque.

As our day at the beach progressed and I enjoyed my vodka and cranberry juice a little too much, I decided to leave the group and walk down the bike path to another beach house where some of my friends were also partying.

Peter is the most nonjealous person in the world. He couldn't have cared less that I left. If he was to ever catch me sitting on an NBA player's lap, he'd probably introduce himself and ask about getting box seats at the Staples Center.

The other party was filled with hot shirtless guys and skinny bitchy girls. I had some more drinks, laughed, flirted, and then headed back to our party for dinner. I continued to be my charming, funny self until dinner was served. We all sat down to barbecued chicken and corn on the cob, when somebody poured me a big goblet of Chardonnay. (Little tip: Do not drink Chardonnay after consuming numerous vodka drinks in the blazing hot sun.)

Halfway through the dinner, my eyes started to roll back into my head and I could no longer form sentences with words from *Webster's*. Wendy, the hostess, said to me, "Let's walk down to the shore and watch the fireworks." When I got up, I could barely stand. My skinny calves were as wobbly as a baby colt just being birthed and attempting to get its footing for the very first time.

Later, Peter told me that he and Tim had to basically carry me to his Expedition and place me in it before the fireworks even began. Then as we were driving home on the 405 freeway, I rolled down the window and puked. At 60 miles per hour, the vomit ended up decorating the side of Peter's Expedition like a Jackson Pollock painting. Priceless!

The next morning, I woke up feeling completely humiliated. I had tried to impress Peter's brother and instead ended up looking like a total lush. Out of my hangover blur, I sat on the step that divided the living room from the dining room in his condo and asked, "Where is this going?"

Can you believe after my performance the previous night I had the audacity to ask where this relationship was going? I'm surprised he didn't respond, "It's going to the car wash. Do you not know what you did to my Expedition?"

Instead, he said, "Well, who knows where anything is going, but I love you and we'll see."

I apologized and insisted that I must have been "rufied" at the other party. What else could explain my behavior? When Peter brought up the fact that people who are slipped "rufies" pass out almost immediately and are not conscious enough to vomit, I suggested maybe it was food poisoning. I told him how I get food poisoning all the time.

I told him how once I went to a really good French restaurant and had about seven drinks and some chicken crepes and got totally sick. I don't know how the restaurant was rated, but obviously something was wrong with their food that night. What else would explain my illness? They had great drinks but very sick food.

When I realized I was not going to win my argument, I asked for Peter's keys and took his car to the car wash. When I got there, I told them how my boyfriend got so sick last night and puked out the window as I was driving him home. "Isn't he disgusting?"

I had told a similar lie at the dry cleaners when bringing in the minidress with vomit on it. I said, "This is my sister's. We just dropped her off at rehab. I'd like to have it clean for her when she gets home."

The woman said, "Oh, OK. Next Friday OK?"

"No, I need this by Thursday," I replied. She looked at me suspiciously, so I went on sincerely: "It's visiting day and I want to show her that her last horrible binge-drinking episode did not ruin her favorite dress. Please. It will really lift her spirits if she could wear a Lycra tube dress to group."

Peter and I continued to date and fell deeper in love. I managed not to get rufied, food poisoning, or overly drunk for months, which was a miracle for me.

He would say things to me like, "Wouldn't you like to get a little house?" And we would both talk about how we wanted kids someday.

About nine months into our relationship, we went to visit my sister Shannon and her husband in Palm Desert for the weekend. After dinner, Peter was acting really dickish and being argumentative with my sister and me. When we went to our room, I tried to save the evening by attempting to get romantic, but he got all annoyed and rejected me, so I asked him what was going on. He said, "I just don't want to get anyone pregnant."

"I know," I said. "That's why I'm on the pill."

"Well, someone is saying that I am the father of her child," he stated.

My first thought was that this child was a year and a half old. I don't know why—that is just what popped in my head. So I asked, "How old is this child?"

He got all flustered and said, "It's not born yet."

What the fuck! Had Peter been cheating on me? He went on to say that the weekend before he met me at Jamie's birthday party, he met a woman named Linda, they went on one date, and had sex. He then went on a date with me a few days later and decided to blow her off for me. He had not seen her since. He told me that she phoned him to say that he was the father of the baby, which was due in about a month.

I thought I was going to faint. All my dreams of my perfect future were shattering before me.

Peter said he'd wanted to tell me, but he kept chickening out.

I could see why. Needless to say, the weekend was ruined. I asked what Linda was like. He said she was thirty-five and a hairdresser. Every hairdresser I've had has been very cool and artsy, usually sporting a few tattoos and always changing her hair color. He said she lived in Orange County and owned her own condo.

I began with my firing line of typical questions. "What does she look like?"

"She's Asian," Peter said tentatively.

"Oh my God! The baby is not even going to look like me," I cried. I kept thinking about how everything now had changed and would never be the same. I cried and I cried until I fell asleep.

I woke up the next morning like most people do after a tragedy. Your first thought is, Oh, it's morning, and then the dread sets in. Wait—did last night happen or was it a nightmare?

Yes, it was real. I know it can't be compared to a death, but it felt like the death of our relationship.

There was a glimmer of hope that this might not be his child. We would find out after DNA tests were done, but Peter said he felt in his soul that it was his child. He told me that he had seen a lawyer to find out his rights and responsibilities and that he was going to be part of this child's life, but that he would understand if I wanted to break up with him.

I went through the timeline and knew he was telling the truth about when this child was conceived. There is a possibility that the conception may have happened that Thursday night, because he said he had plans and asked if I'd like to go out on our first date on Wednesday or Friday. Had I chosen Wednesday, would it have gone so well that he would have canceled his Thursday night date with Linda?

He told me that she had contacted him once before when she first found out she was pregnant. Once it was established that she was keeping the baby, he told her that he had a girlfriend and was not interested in her romantically. She stopped calling. Then a month ago, she called again and said she was due to give birth soon, and that's when he went to see an attorney.

We went on with our Sunday. All the while, I pretended to my sister and brother-in-law that nothing was wrong. The whole day, I had a big pit in my stomach and I just kept thinking about the situation. What was going to happen? I have always loved children and never had a fear of being a stepmother or even one day adopting. I knew if we were to stay together, I could love this child like my own.

I thought of the benefits of my potential stepmother role. Unlike being with a man who was married with a child, I would never have to compete with the child knowing her biological parents as having been together. I processed all of this information. That night I presented Peter with a letter telling him that I was going to stay with him and support him in this, no matter what the outcome might be. I did have the good sense not to share this with any friends or family. I felt we had to know the DNA outcome before I told anyone. Also, I didn't want my friends bashing him behind my back. Peter was a thirty-three-year-old man who chose to have sex and not use a condom, and the result was a child.

About two weeks later, I hadn't heard from Peter all day and I kept calling and calling him. Whenever I start to worry about someone, my mind leaps to the worst possible scenario, death. I still do that today. I think which black dress I would wear for the funeral and what I would wear to the Rosary the night before. Would I go with a Diane von Furstenberg black wrap dress or stick with my tried-and-true black Theory pant-suit. Obviously, we'd have Brent's Deli cater the wake (otherwise known as the "after party"). Hmm. Now, would we go with little premade sandwiches or do a meat and assorted cheese plate so that people could conveniently make their own? I would be crying so much that I would definitely not go with false eyelashes that day, but would I do full Jackie-O sunglasses?

I was broken from my paranoid planning by the ringing of the telephone. It was Peter.

"Where have you been all day?" I demanded, hoping I sounded more concerned than bitchy.

Before I could ask if he preferred little premade sandwiches on a variety of breads or a make-your-own-sandwich kind of platter should I ever have to plan his wake, he said, "Well you got your wish."

"What are you talking about?" I asked.

"It's a girl. I'm at the hospital." He sounded excited. My stomach dropped. I had forgotten, of course, that about two weeks ago I told him that I had hoped it was a girl, because I thought it would be easier for a single mother to raise a daughter.

Oh God! The man I want to spend the rest of my life with just had his first child with someone else. I burst into tears and hung up on him.

I immediately called Tara and told her everything. She has called me in tears numerous times throughout our friendship, but this was the first time she had to console me. I was a blubbering emotional mess. She was at my apartment in ten minutes. She basically said Peter wasn't for me, that he should have told me back when he first heard from Linda regarding the pregnancy, and that I could do better. As she hugged me goodbye, I swore her to secrecy.

Peter called. He sounded exhausted. He said one of Linda's friends called him to say she had the baby, so he went to the hospital and took pictures and everything. Peter did the right thing. Like all fathers, he should take pictures, but it just made me feel even more insecure. I told him I needed him to come over, and he did. He held me and fell asleep in a matter of minutes.

The next morning, he said that they did the DNA test and that it would take two weeks to get the results, but he just knew that the baby was his daughter.

I was writing and acting on a TV show at the time, *Lyricist Lounge,* and I shared the whole story with two of the other writers: a single mom and a married father. Both of them told me to run for the hills. They said I was young and on a TV show. Sure, the show was on MTV, but they still felt I could do better and should not sign up for this. But all I could think about was if I dumped Peter, I just knew within a year another girl would be in the passenger seat of that Expedition having a great life with him, while I would still be dating assholes and living with a crazy roommate.

I looked at the situation as if I was Saint Joseph, when Mary, mother of Jesus, had to tell Joseph, her fiancé, that she was pregnant by someone other than him. Saint Joseph married her anyway, and he's the most famous stepfather in the world. Sure, Peter's baby mama is not the Lord. She's a Vietnamese hair-and-nail lady in California, and this is not taking place in Bethlehem. But other than that, the similarities are eerie.

What was a good Catholic like me to do but marry her pregnant boyfriend, except that the baby had already been born?

I decided to think of the positive things. There was just the one baby; it's not like Linda gave birth to octuplets. She was healthy, and Asian babies have never been more in style. Plus, they're traditionally overachievers at math. Also, what if I couldn't have kids? This may be my only chance to be an almost mother.

That night, Peter and I went to dinner and we basically decided to get married. He never really asked me, but there was no way in hell I was going to go through this as "the girlfriend." I can't say for sure if there is a rule regarding your boyfriend's getting another woman pregnant in *The Rules,* but I'm pretty sure the authors would agree I broke it.

I was in the room when Peter called his mother, Ginny, and said, "Congratulations, you're a grandmother again."

At first, she thought I was pregnant. She never got around to guessing that it was a woman he met at an El Torino happy hour in Riverside County nine months earlier. Maybe those dollar margaritas weren't such a great deal, after all. He made plans to meet Ginny at the hospital in Fullerton the following morning and to introduce her to Linda and to her new grand-daughter, Mackenzie.

Peter made plans to take his mother to meet Mackenzie (that was the baby's name). I then told Peter that I wanted to go to the hospital with him, to show Linda that I had no resent-ment toward her or the baby and that I was there to help when Peter had his visitations.

When I got to the hospital, Peter introduced me. Linda, an attractive woman, even just after giving birth, wouldn't look at me. I walked over to Ginny, who was now holding Mackenzie, and I touched the baby's tiny hand. Just then, the nurse said Linda wanted me to leave. I ran out of the hospital room crying and Peter followed me, trying to assure me that everything was going to be OK. I guess Linda didn't appreciate my being there.

During the numerous custody hearings to follow, this in-cident kept coming up, making Peter look like a total asshole. Once a judge questioned his judgment, he declared, "You, Mr. All American, take your current girlfriend to your former girl-friend's hospital room, just after she gave birth to your child?" Yes, in retrospect, it did look bad.

• • •

What followed during the next five years were custody battles and false accusations to fuel a Lifetime Saturday movie marathon. In anticipation of yet another fight with her mother we would video tape Mackenzie's feedings on our weekends with her. I would say into the video camera, "Hello, it's Saturday morning at nine-oh-eight a.m. and this is Gerber's organic bananas Level Two." Linda fought every settlement that was presented to her. It wasn't enough money. Then she wanted Peter to pay for her to go to computer technology school. All the while, the attorney bills were piling up.

Once I had decided I was going to spend the rest of my life with Peter, I told my parents. I went to their house for dinner and announced I had some news.

My mom looked up and said, "You're getting married?"

"Well, yes, but . . ."

Before I could finish, my dad interrupted, "You're pregnant?"

"No, but Peter was," I said.

They both looked at me rather confused. Then I explained to them that Peter had gotten knocked up and I was going to make an honest man out of him by marrying him. I told the whole story of Linda and Mackenzie, as well as the problems we were having with settling on a visitation schedule and child support.

My dad suggested Peter just pay to support the child but relinquish his parental rights. He said this woman was going to make our lives hell. In his day, this was a respectable option, but Peter was going to be an active father to his child and that is what I loved most about him.

During all of this, Peter and I started planning our wedding. Only my parents, Shannon, and Tara knew about Mackenzie. We were having a big wedding with 170 guests. I didn't want to be in the bathroom stall at my wedding reception and overhear guests whispering, "You know, he has a baby with someone else, not even an ex-wife. It's a mess. I would never marry someone with that kind of baggage. I'm glad I got the chicken; the salmon smelled very fishy." That is why I chose not to tell my other sister, Kathi, who would go crazy over this juicy story.

In order to get married in our Catholic church, you have to go through an eight-hour pre-cana seminar/workshop, take a personality test, and then meet with another couple to discuss the results of the test. I think this is important. The seminar was a lot like traffic school. It takes place on a Saturday; you meet new people, break into small groups, and eat a box lunch of a turkey sandwich, potato chips, and a chocolate chip cookie.

At one point, they had us add up all of our personal debt and tell the group what it was. The instructor's opinion was that a couple should not get married if one person is bringing excess debt into the marriage. I looked at Peter's paper. Despite the lawyers' fees, he had no debt besides his mortgage and a car payment. He had no credit card debt.

I broke down and cried to the group: "Yes, I am eighteen thousand dollars in credit card debt! But that is it! My parents paid for my schooling at USC. I have no student loans.

Shouldn't that stand for something? I was in The Groundlings theater for years. We performed comedy sketches. I had to buy wigs and costumes and get new head shots every few years. I had to buy spaghetti strap sundresses that I couldn't afford so that I could attract a guy like Peter. So there, burn me at the stake, I lived beyond my means in my twenties!"

Everyone was shocked by my honest outburst. However, Peter was very understanding. It was yet another benefit to having my fiancé father another woman's baby. It made my little old eighteen grand in credit card debt look like mere pennies.

The next thing we had to do to get married in the church was to meet with the couple about our personality compatibility test. We went to Debbie and Don's home. I had known them for years because I went to grammar and high school with their daughters. Their eldest daughter had just gotten her marriage annulled, but Don was very proud of himself because he had his suspicions from the start and therefore never changed his daughter's trust to include the husband. All I could think of at the time was, I wish I had a trust.

As we started to talk, Don said, "Now, I see you have a child, Peter. Do you support it?"

"Yes," Peter answered.

"Good," Don and Debbie replied in unison.

I said, "She's seven months old."

"Seven months old!" Debbie screeched. "I thought you were going to say seven years old."

I started to cry and told them the whole story. I wanted to get everything out and tell them everything we had been through, to really use this as a useful counseling session for us as a couple. As we left, I felt great about it. I had purged all my fears and frustrations.

This was a Friday night. The following Monday morning, my phone rang at work. It was Debbie.

She said, "Well, Don and I prayed for you all weekend long, and we know the invitations have gone out and deposits have been paid, but we really feel you should postpone your wedding. We just feel that Peter has everything to gain by marrying you and you have everything to lose."

Oh my God! Now I felt bad that I had ruined two people's weekend with them worrying about me the whole time when she could have been making her famous chocolate mint bars and he could have been golfing.

"Debbie, I appreciate your thoughts, but to be honest with you, I am not as happening as you may think. Peter is the best guy I've ever met and I'm eighteen thousand dollars in credit card debt. I failed to tell you that," I confessed.

"Well, dear, in our evaluation we could not recommend to Monsignor that you get married, and I still think you should really think about it and what your future might be like with this man."

I immediately called Peter and told him how they thought I shouldn't marry him.

He asked, "Well, did you tell them about your eighteen thousand dollars of credit card debt?"

"Yes, I did tell them, and she still told me I could do better," I said proudly. I still love reminding Peter of this a few times a year. Every time I see this couple at church, I make sure they see us, and how cute we are. Debbie has to fight back tears of joy each time. I really think she, as a mother, was worried for me, since she was coming off her own daughter's failed marriage. Needless to say, we continued with our wedding plans and Monsignor never said a dang thing, which made me wonder if he even read those long typewritten reports that Don and Debbie had agonized and prayed over before writing.

The next on our marriage to-do's was getting Peter fitted for a tuxedo. That day, we had Mackenzie with us. I loved how people complimented on how amazing I looked for just giving birth. I would just thank them and pat my tummy.

I also loved how they looked at Peter like, "You're doing the right thing man, marrying this girl." I mean, is there anything more Hollywood than the cute actress marrying the baby's daddy after the baby is born and able to attend the nuptials?

Peter's father, Joe, who passed away in 2004, had a very matter-of-fact attitude about the whole thing. He had lived through World War II in Czechoslovakia and seen many atrocities. When I asked him what he thought when he first heard about Peter's becoming a father, he answered, "I thought, well, it's about time. I was surprised it didn't happen sooner."

What the hell does that mean? Apparently, Peter had a lot of girlfriends.

About a year ago when Tom Brady left his pregnant actress girlfriend Bridget Moynahan for supermodel Gisele Bündchen, I really could relate. I, of course, was the supermodel in this scenario. People thought Tom Brady was terrible for doing this, but obviously he was not in love with Bridget. Had he married her, he would be doing her no favors. Gisele's mistake, however, was telling *Vanity Fair* that she felt she was just as much the baby boy's mother as if she had given birth to him herself. First of all, it's not wrong to think that, but even if Gisele did think it, why would she tell *Vanity Fair*? You'd think after being a Victoria's Secret model all these years, she would have learned how to keep a damn secret.

As Mackenzie grew to be a toddler and was looking a little more Asian, we'd get approached usually by older couples inquiring where we got her. Once an older woman came up to me at a restaurant and said, "She's adorable. Our daughter went all the way to China to get hers."

It took everything in me not to say, "Really? That's far. My husband just had to go to a happy hour in Fullerton to get ours."

Once we were married, things with Linda only got worse, and our attorney recommended that in order to avoid any more false accusations, we should start doing the exchanges at the police department. At the precinct in the West Valley, they even have a special little section with toys for the children to play with. It's interesting to see the dads and the kids at the police department on Friday nights and Sunday afternoons. Ah, what a wonderful society we live in. Who knew that one day the police would be here to serve, protect, and babysit? Today, Mackenzie is ten, and thankfully the last couple of years have been very uneventful. We do exchanges at Starbucks now, where the coffee is better and served in more environmentally friendly cups.

When Mackenzie was around four years old and we would

read the princess stories, it was a little awkward for me that the stepmother character was always so evil. I don't know what went down in Walt Disney's childhood, but I'm guessing he didn't call his stepmother "Mommy." Snow White and Cinderella ruined it for any stepmother trying to get in good with her boyfriend's preschooler. Once when we were reading fairy tales, Mackenzie said, "You're a mean stepmother."

"Well, you know, that is not true," I said calmly.

Mackenzie giggled and said, "It's a joke, because it's not true." Even though that is not the proper definition of a joke by the official joke rule book, it made it clear that to Mackenzie I was not an evil stepmother and that was all that mattered.

 **The AARPs Next Door**

Today my life is pretty darn fantastic. Peter and I are still married and will celebrate our tenth wedding anniversary this year. Mackenzie is also ten and in the fifth grade.

Yes, I have vaginally given birth to two boys—Drake, who is seven, and Brandon, who is four years old. Because I only gave birth to boys I feel that much more blessed to be a stepmother to such a beautiful daughter who is calm and likes to shop at the American Girl store. Praise the Lord that they have not come up with an American Boy store because then I'd really be screwed. Hot Wheels are not nearly as expensive. Mackenzie's and my shopping sprees come complete with visiting the doll hospital, which unfortunately does not take Blue Cross but does take AmEx, and a hair salon that Vidal Sassoon himself would be proud to put his name on. They should have an American Girl Bank so parents can get a second mortgage to pay for all of the dresses, accessories, beds, nightstands, dressers, and little stuffed pets. I love that Mackenzie is still innocent. When she wanted to buy Addy a girl from the 1800s, I simply didn't know how I felt about my daughter owning a doll who was a slave.

Having a daughter who is ten can be a wake-up call for me too, like when my cleaning lady keeps mistakenly placing my clothes in Mackenzie's closet. I get it, Margarita; my dresses are a little short for my age. Thanks for the subtle hint.

A few years ago we bought the 1960s ranch-style house next door to my parents'. They rode the real estate wave all the way until this latest bust in 2007 and now I feel they watch way too much TV. Why is everyone concerned with how much TV their children watch yet no one thinks that watching Fox News for twenty-four hours straight may not the best thing for senior citizens to do with their life?

To some, choosing to live next door to one's parents may sound crazy, but so far it's truly been great. They have a heated pool and we don't, so we built a little gate between our two houses and we are able to go swimming whenever we want. Sure, it's a little awkward when we have big pool parties in their backyard and they aren't invited and I see them staring at us, with their noses pressed against the French doors, but I think they understand that the same friends who accidentally witnessed my dad skinny-dipping in our pool at my fourth-grade slumber party don't want to see him to do it again at eighty, wearing only a pair of goggles and flippers. My parents are great when I need a babysitter, or run out of milk or Chardonnay. My mom always has an ice-cold bottle waiting ready to be uncorked, or if we really need a Vicodin, it's convenient to have relatives with a senior prescription plan right smack next door.

I am also really grateful that I did not listen to some of my friends who told me not to marry Peter because of all of his baby baggage, especially because those same friends are still single today.

The one friend whose advice I sought and took was Regan, who is fifteen years older than I am. She had given me great advice before about whether or not I should go two thousand dollars deeper into debt by taking three different planes on New Year's Eve to be a bridesmaid in my sorority sister's wedding. Her advice was: Don't be a bridesmaid. At twenty-five it was all about being a good friend and worrying that my other friends would think I was a bad friend for not participating. Regan was like having Dr. Phil and Suze Orman rolled into one attractive heterosexual female. She had the maturity to explain to me that invites to destination weddings are something you can turn down, especially if you are a poor, struggling girl in her twenties. So, based on my financial situation, I legally had an out, and after a lovely letter and generous gift to the bride, we are still friends today. Besides, the dress was tea length—the absolute worst cut for my tiny ankles. It would have looked like two toothpicks coming out of a large marshmallow. So when I explained the Peter situation to her, she immediately said, "This might be the greatest thing to happen to you." She went on to say, "What if this is the only child you are ever able to have—won't you be grateful that you could be a stepmother to a healthy daughter?" When I remind her now of all the good advice she has given me in my life she just laughs and says, "Well, I'm glad I was able to give such good advice to you because I certainly haven't given it to myself."

I don't ever want to be that married woman who brags about how strong her marriage is, because I always think of the woman who wrote *The Rules for Marriage* and then just as the book was about to hit the stands it was announced that she was getting divorced. Whenever a couple I know, either personally or in the public eye, breaks up it makes me sad because no matter how confident you are it reminds you that every relationship is vulnerable—including your own.

Nothing was more heartbreaking than when Jesse James cheated repeatedly on America's sweetheart, Sandy Bullock. How could he do that to her, especially after she took that poor black boy into her home and taught him how to play football? What made it worse was that in the months prior, every interview and every speech Sandra gave including when she won the Oscar was about how wonderful her husband was. This is why I purposely don't say that many nice things about Peter—it's a curse, because if you do, the next thing you find out is your husband's been fucking a tattooed Nazi.

Having now written a book while being married I empathize with the author of *The Rules for Marriage*. Working full-time at *Chelsea Lately* and performing stand-up comedy around the country and into foreign territory like Canada allowed me only the weekends to write this book. As much as I truly enjoyed remembering these stories and laughing out loud as I typed, as I arrived home at seven p.m. on Friday night I'd start getting anxious about all the work ahead of me. Soon I'd become more and more resentful that Peter was going to golf with his slightly overweight, middle-aged friends on Saturday mornings. To say the least, a few fights were had. I'd say, "Why can't you stay home and help with the kids?" And he'd say, "But the nanny is coming tomorrow so you won't have to be disturbed." And I would say, "What's so fun about golf anyway? I don't think you really love me."

Clearly, any woman would agree, I was in the right. But being married with kids also helps take the drama out of relationships. When it's just the two of you and your man pisses you off, you can cry, grab your keys, and run off in the rain (provided it's raining), and go to your single girlfriend's house, drink wine, and tell each other how great you both are. But when you've got kids depending on you, it's different. I often ask myself, How long am I going to let this argument go? Do I really want to pack a bag and sleep at the Woodland Hills Marriot or Comfort Inn? Because my single girlfriends are now married and I don't want to go to their house and end up taking care of their kids. I think our longest period of not talking—besides when I'm watching a *Real Housewives* or a *Keeping Up with the Kardashians* marathon—is about twenty minutes. Besides, we both like our king-size Tempur-Pedic mattress topper with our fourteen goose down pillows too much, so even sleeping somewhere else separately doesn't happen much.

We are not strangers to marriage counseling, either. However, we've only been three times. On the third session Peter admitted he was wrong to yell at me about the crumbs in his car from the poppy seed cake and after that we stopped booking therapy sessions. Now all I have to do is to threaten for us to go again and he whips right back into shape.

Through the years, our marriage has gone through some changes. In the beginning I was still acting like a contestant on *The Bachelor,* pretending I was that sport-loving low-maintenance chick who's up for anything. In the first three years of being married I rode an ATV, slept on a small rocking boat in the Galápagós Islands for seven nights, and attempted to ride a bicycle above the clouds of the Haleakala volcano down the road from Hana Maui at five a.m. because that way we could really enjoy the sunrise. Now when Peter makes those kinds of suggestions, I simply say, "No, thank you, go without me. I just booked a massage." That way, we are both much happier.

Recently, Peter and I decided to purchase some furniture. The designer from the store met us at our house at seven in the evening, and as the hours passed on I became more and more exhausted and just wanted her to leave. I started to agree to everything she pointed at in the catalog and began to write her a huge deposit check. When Peter objected, saying we should go to the store and at least sit on the furniture once, I said, "No, we have to give her a check now. That's how she said it works." The next morning I came to my senses and canceled my $16,000 check to the furniture store and for the first time I had a better understanding of how innocent people confess to murders they did not commit after they've endured hours of police interrogation. After further discussion, Peter and I did put in a furniture order. However, making purchasing decisions can cause problems between Peter and me because I'll think we've made a joint decision, yet when something goes wrong with the purchase, suddenly I'm the only one who wanted the new ceiling fan. So, to prevent future arguments like the one I predict that will happen the day my son spills his milk on our new couch and Peter screams, "I told you we should have gone with leather, but no, you wanted cloth," I can whip out a contract I had a lawyer friend of mine put together that Peter signed, stating: "I, Peter James Dobias, do hereby, and with free volition swear, affirm, agree, and aver that the decision to make the furniture purchase of January 12, 2010, and the specifics of size, color, and upholstery attendant to said purchase, was made equally and with full agreement by the party of the first part, Peter James Dobias, and the party of the second part, Heather Ann McDonald. Should any breach of this agreement occur, contemplating the difficulty of determining the value of damage this would incur to the marriage, child rearing, and homemaking of the parties, damages shall be paid in the amount of one one-hundred-dollar Nordstrom's gift card per violation. Signed in the Year of Our Lord 2010, Peter Dobias."

It's little preventive measures like this that have helped keep me sane—that and choosing to never take my children to restaurants that involve waiters. I'm the first to admit that the only green food my boys eat are their own boogers.

Being a working mom is not easy. That's why my motto is not "having it all" but rather "having it most," because once you become a mother to something other than an animal you simply can't have it all but you can try to have most of it. You can't decide to lie in bed hungover all day and read a *Vanity Fair* from front to back because at seven a.m. someone is screaming for cereal and you can only say "five more minutes" so many times before your child climbs on your head and begins to jump up and down. When you're hungover this is really unpleasant.

I am far from the perfect mom. That is why I rely on a good Catholic school to whip my boys into shape. They attend the same Catholic school I went to, which I loved. In fact, when the nuns and the priests used to talk about receiving the "calling" to devote their lives to Christ, I wanted to do the right thing. Still every time the phone rang I was petrified that it was going to be Jesus on the other end asking for me and I had just seen a movie about a woman becoming a nun and there was a scene where the priest cuts off all her long gorgeous hair on the altar, a priest mind you, not even a licensed beautician. So I promised Jesus that I would become a nun but only after I got married, had all my children, and my husband died. Then when I was say, sixty-years-old, I'd be happy to sport a short hairdo, move into the convent, giggle with all the other sisters in the garden, and drive my nun car around. (At my parish, they all drove white Toyota Tercels. Some big donor must have owned a dealership.) I was never more relieved than when it was explained to me that "the calling" does not involve AT&T or their long distance plan to heaven.

Being a parent at the same school I attended is a little déjà vu, because during teacher-parent conferences I am in some of the exact same classrooms I was in thirty years ago and I get that familiar pit in my stomach. At the last one the teacher said great things about Drake, but then she said the "only thing is," he was late eight times this semester. The "only thing" he failed at had to do solely with me. Though at seven he is extremely advanced, he can't drive himself, so when she said that about being late it was pretty hard for me to try to pass the blame but I still managed to do so by blaming my husband, saying that he's the one who drives them every morning.

Sexually, my husband still couldn't care less that I was virgin until I was twenty-seven except that it resulted in a book deal. We have a good sex life; at least I believe we do. Another great thing about having very few partners and experience is that I don't have much to compare it to so I don't know any better. I often have sexual dreams where someone other than my husband is hitting on me and in the dream I say to myself, "Look, you and I both know this is a dream, so it's not adultery—just go for it." Infidelity when it is confined to dreams or Lifetime movies is not considered a mortal sin by the Catholic Church.

I'm happy that people can't come out of the woodwork and say I was bad in bed. Even today, with many years of experience under my belt, I don't think I'm amazing in bed. To be perfectly honest, Peter and I are your average bread-and-butter boners. When it comes to viewing porn it consists of HBO original programming and a little Cinemax, which results mostly in my husband and me arguing about which street in the San Fernando Valley we believe the film was shot on. I do however love to fantasize. My favorite is to come up with scenarios featuring my husband but at a time when I was still virginal. One summer day after we went swimming and the kids were watching *The Polar Express* in the playroom, I said to Peter, "OK, let's pretend it's nineteen ninety-seven and we're at a pool party in the Hollywood Hills. We've been drinking all day in the hot sun, and we're just meeting now waiting in line for the bathroom, let's do this." Or we play doctor and I pretend I don't have insurance. Sometimes it works out and sometimes Peter gets frustrated by it all. He's not an actor so he's not great with the improvisation, and he doesn't stick to strong character choices, which are all necessary if we're going to bring things to a climactic point. But who am I kidding, *The Polar Express* does eventually end or the DVD skips, at which point sexy time is immediately over.

The best conversations I have with my husband today are when he is driving us for a weekend trip a few hours away. Even though we are interrupted a few times to pass a juice box back, for the most part we can really talk and I love that. The other weekend on our way to Palm Desert I asked Peter, "If I died and all of my friends were single, which one would you marry?" Peter said, "I'm not going to answer that." To which I replied, "Come on, if you died I know which one of your friends I'd marry." He then gave a big sigh and said, "Heather, if you died, I would never ever get married again. . . . I'm just so goddamn tired." Well, that is not a compliment but at least I have the comfort in knowing that Peter will never marry again thanks to what I've put him through.

Just today my mother-in-law sent me a photo she took in our driveway last weekend and in the photo there was a beautiful girl, two cute boys on bikes, a Lexus, and a white picket fence. Wow, all my dreams really have come true!

Being a virgin well into one's twenties isn't for everyone. It never paid my rent or got me free trips to Hawaii, but I don't regret any decisions I've made and feel very blessed to be where I am today.

On this season of *The Bachelor: On the Wings of Love* with the dorky bubble-butt airline pilot, he was down to five girls and one confessed to him that she was a twenty-three-year-old virgin. She went on to explain that she is still very sexual and that it doesn't define her and he told her he thought it was great and then that night at the rose ceremony, guess who got the boot, the virgin. No rose for the girl with the scarlet V on her cocktail dress. My advice to her would be not to tell the next guy too soon, but seeing as how she just announced it on national television, that might be difficult. So instead I'd like to say to that *Bachelor* contestant and any other cute, attractive virgin in her twenties out there, be true to yourself and blue ball until you don't want to blue ball anymore!

 Acknowledgments

I would like to first thank Chelsea Handler, the most generous performer I know, for hiring me to write on her show, *Chelsea Lately,* and all the stand-up gigs, vacations, shoes, sushi, cocktails, and general perks that come along with being one of her employees—and, more important, from her friendship. I'd also like to thank Chelsea for introducing me to my agent, Michael Broussard, the best in the business.

I'd like to give special thanks to my sister Shannon, for always being there, from driving me to a seniors-only party to lying on my bed laughing as we watch our kids play together. Also thank you to all my family, which includes the rest of the McDonalds, The Dobiases, The McAvoys, The Careys, and anyone else in Ireland who is somehow related to my father, Bob McDonald.

To the best mother-in-law in the world, Virginia Dobias,

thank you for taking care of my children and raising my husband.

To my husband, Peter, and my children, Mackenzie, Drake, and Brandon, thank you for making my dream of being a wife and mother a reality.

To my two best friends—Elizabeth Killmond Roman, whom I met in first grade when her desk was moved next to mine at St. Mel Catholic School, and Tara Klein, whom I met at my high school entrance exam at Louisville High School— and to all of my other girlfriends and sorority sisters I met at USC, especially Maia Dreyer and Stacey Jenks for making my life so much fun and for always encouraging me to follow my dreams.

To my editor, Zachary Schisgal, to Stacey Creamer, and to everyone else at Simon & Schuster Touchstone Fireside who helped make this book so great. To Bernie Cahill and Jordan Tilzer at Roar; Sandy and Brian at The McCabe Group, and Stephen Bender and Sue Carswell for all their help.

To my friends and coworkers at *Chelsea Lately,* especially Guy Branum, Tom Brunelle, Sue Murphy, Chris Franjola, Steve Marmalstein, Jen Kirkman, Chuy Bravo, Sarah Colonna, Brad Wollack, Jeff Wild, and Johnny Milord—thank you for making the last three years of my life hilarious. Also to Jillian Barberie-Reynolds and the Kardashian-Jenner clan for being so supportive of my career. And to the Wayans Brothers especially to Keenen, Shawn, and Marlon who have hired me numerous times. Yes, the black man has been very good to me.

And to all of my friends, whether real, or in cyberspace on

MySpace, Facebook, and Twitter, thank you for coming to my shows and for buying this book.

Finally, to my parents, Bob and Pam, thank you for sacrificing so much for me and for paying for twelve years of private Catholic education and for footing the bill for four years at The University of Southern California solely because I said if you didn't let me go there I would get depressed every time I saw a USC license plate frame. See, it was worth it! Also for loving me unconditionally and bragging about me every chance you get. I love you both!